Spike Lee

AND THE AFRICAN AMERICAN FILMMAKERS

SPIKE LEE

and
the
African American
Filmmakers:
A Choice
of Colors

K. MAURICE JONES

The Millbrook Press
Brookfield, Connecticut

Photographs courtesy and © IPA/Stills/Retna Ltd.: p. 15; John Kisch, Separate Cinema Archive, Hyde Park, N.Y.: pp. 19, 31; Photofest: pp. 21, 30, 33, 37, 39, 46, 56, 61, 67, 83, 86, 88, 116, 127; UPI/Bettmann: p. 24; Frank Driggs Collection: p. 28; Jim Wilson, New York Times Pictures: p. 52; Frank Stewart: p. 72; Universal City Studios, Inc: pp. 74, 102; Warner Bros.: p. 92; Gramercy Pictures: p. 105; Anthony Barboza: pp. 110, 124, 134; Columbia Pictures: p. 111; Hollywood Pictures Company: p. 113; Tristar Pictures: p. 120; Twentieth Century Fox: p. 129.

Library of Congress Cataloging-in-Publication Data
Jones, K. Maurice.
Spike Lee and the African American filmmakers : a choice of colors / K. Maurice Jones.
p.   cm.
Includes bibliographical references and index.
Summary: Surveys African American filmmakers from the turn of the century to the present, with an emphasis on Spike Lee's contributions.
ISBN 1-56294-518-1 (lib. bdg.)
1. Lee, Spike—Criticism and interpretation—Juvenile literature. 2. Afro-American motion picture producers and directors—United States—Juvenile literature. 3. Afro-Americans in the motion picture industry—United States—Juvenile literature. [1. Lee, Spike. 2. Motion picture producers and directors. 3. Afro-Americans—Biography.] I. Title.
PN1998.3.L44J66   1996
791.43'0233'08996073—dc20   96-4851   CIP   AC

Published by The Millbrook Press, Inc.
2 Old New Milford Road
Brookfield, Connecticut 06804

Respect to the pillars:
Jean, William, Miss Eddie Mae,
Harry Lewis, Sister Myrtis Jones, Hightower,
and the Reverend James Edward Wadsworth.

And to Adebola.

X Amount of Niceness to the late Dora Harper; Anthony Williams; Matt Robinson; Dr. Michael Eric Dyson; Savion Glover; Woodlawn; Teri Kane; Ray Phiri; Gerald and Eddie Levert; Home Box Office; Djibrill Diallo; Virginia Wadsworth; Denise Stinson; Donna Williams; Kim Jack Riley; the Scholastic Black Caucus; Eldad-Medad; The Warrior Council; Fellowship Chapel; Dr. Johnny Ray Youngblood; the Reverend Wendell Anthony; Ceciliaville; Shawn Rhea; Dinwiddie-Boyd; George Pitts (my hero); Kevin Powell (Stagger Lee); Narada Michael Walden; Antonio Sharp; A. Wayne Anderson; Eli Fountain; Geoffrey Jacques; Galen T. Pauling; Darren Nichols; Ann Hass; Gabriel's Griots; the inspiring Adetokunbo Adelekan; Professor Quincy Troupe; the Fraser Family; Adis Channer; Dr. Waldo Johnson; JW; J. Gaines; Karen Gault; Kathy Gerhardt; Sheila and Sandra Lee Jamison; Enna Jones; Colin Channer; Ever Cool; Juanita Burton; Douglas Keene; Sal Principato; Brenda Jackson; Themba Sibeko; Pam Mitchell; Mike Cash; George Norfleet; Tonya Steele; Donna Williams; Gail Hamilton; Charles Watts; Steve Holsey; Greg Dunmore; Charles Lewis; the Minister of Information; Anthony Lewis; Alfred Jackson; Preston Whitmore; Baba Tunji; Sumurah; Beans; Tonya Reeves; One Son; the Reverend Opal Simmons; Narcelle Reedus; JEH; Men Who Read; the Charles Family; Mike D; Kristin Krueger; the National Film Information Service; Carlford Wadley; J. Green; Celeste Davis; Phyllis Harrell; Maalik Mudenda (soon come); all supporters of *Say It Loud!*; Leroy Hyter; Deborah C, editorial angel; and the ever-patient, ever-visionary Frank Menchaca, editorial ruler; JAH LIVE!

WE HAVE TO SEE EACH OTHER WITH NEW EYES.

Malcolm X, *The Ballot or the Bullet*

THE LANGUAGE OF THE CAMERA IS THE LANGUAGE OF OUR DREAMS.

James Baldwin, *The Devil Finds Work*

CONTENTS

if you had A CHOICE OF COLORS

which one would you choose my brothers?

CURTIS MAYFIELD AND
THE IMPRESSIONS
"A CHOICE OF COLORS"

prologue

A HOT DAY IN NEW YORK CITY

New York is a sweltering concrete jungle. The sun fries the pavement. Buses belch exhaust into the crowded streets. Fans, air conditioners, and gushing fire hydrants provide no relief. From the oldest to the youngest, everyone is held captive to the heat.

Spike Lee is sweating it out in a film-editing room. The air-conditioned studio in the Broadway theater district is high above the inferno. The African American filmmaker is laboring long and hard as he mixes the sound for his screen biography of the charismatic black leader Malcolm X.

Malcolm, played by Denzel Washington, walks across an 84-foot screen. He wears a blue prison uniform and a black ski cap. Baines, a fellow inmate, quietly converses with him. In the background other convicts in the courtyard play baseball. The dialogue between the two prisoners is soul-searching:

Baines: "What's your name, boy?"

Malcolm, startled, answers like a boy: "Little."

Baines: "No. That's the name of the slave-master who owned your family. You don't even know who you are. You're nothing. Less than nothing. A zero. What are you?"[1]

Close shot. Malcolm is wrapped in thought. The image freezes.

"Okay, let's roll it back and bring up their footsteps just a little," Spike says to a technician. "Bring the birds down just a little, too." Lee pushes himself away from the control panels, and collapses his 5-foot-7-inch body into a nearby deep, soft, gray leather chair. Fatigue is deep in his bones. Lee has not slept in several days. Spike Lee is fried.[2]

He yawns and stretches his arms. Lee wears a black-and-white T-shirt that boldly bears the words *Jungle Fever,* his controversial 1990 movie about one of America's biggest taboos: interracial relationships. An ankh hangs from his neck. The cross-like configuration is an Egyptian hieroglyphic. It represents the divine continuation of life from generation to generation. As an African American filmmaker and African American male, Lee upholds lofty artistic and nationalistic obligations. Even at a time like this he doesn't forget that he sees himself as on a mission from God. Lee removes his red X baseball cap. Caps bearing the letter X had been the rage in the African American community since 1990, when Lee triumphantly announced to the world that he would direct the often-postponed feature film biography of Malcolm X, the charismatic minister of the Nation of Islam and human-rights advocate.

On Lee's feet are a pair of Air Jordans, the status sneaker of America. The high-top gym shoes are brand-new; they smell like they just came out of the box. Mars Blackmon, the comic character that Lee played in his first major film, *She's Gotta Have It,* now endorses Air Jordans. Lee has written, directed, and costarred in several Nike commercials that featured basketball deity Michael Jordan, as well as cartoon legend Bugs Bunny. Lee's I-just-got-a-trim-at-the-barbershop face leans to one side. It is obvious that the last thing on Lee's mind is his appearance.

Malcolm X has been the most demanding project that Lee has ever worked on. Seemingly at every juncture Lee has confronted resistance. Many black nationalists—activists advocating black self-reliance—protested that Lee would present a distorted image of Malcolm. They predicted that Lee would center on Malcolm's days as the pimp Detroit Red, his drug use, and his relationships with white women. When the film ran five million dollars over budget, the studio and finance company that were backing the project wanted to seize control of the production. Lee held his ground. He insisted on traveling to Mecca, Saudi Arabia, and South Africa to shoot crucial scenes. Indeed, it had been a long road to this afternoon in the editing room.

"Hey Spike, you wanna go to the Greek restaurant for lunch?" an assistant asks.

"Naw man, I got to go back to Forty Acres after this," Lee answers. Forty Acres and a Mule Filmworks, Lee's production company, is based in the Fort Greene section of Brooklyn where Lee grew up. The company was named after a clause in the Freedmen's Bureau Act of 1865, which promised all newly emancipated Negro adult males a piece of farmland and a mule of their own.

"I'll see you guys tomorrow."

"Cool."[3]

during the six years between 1986 and this day in 1992, Lee's work has made him the most important African American in movies. His films of this period—*She's Gotta Have It, School Daze, Do the Right Thing, Mo' Better Blues, Jungle Fever, Malcolm X*—along with his later films *Crooklyn, Clockers,* and *Girl 6* offer the most extensive vision of the black experience by a single African American filmmaker.

Lee has faithfully made movies that have placed the lives of real black people on the silver screen. By no means, however, is Lee a lone cinematic figure. His breakthrough into the closed society of Hollywood-controlled studio movie making has ushered in an unprecedented era in black filmmaking. Mario Van Peebles, Julie Dash, John Singleton, Robert Townsend, the Hudlin Brothers, the Hughes Brothers, Bill Duke, Rusty Aundiezz, Charles Lane, Matty Rich, and others have joined him to create a new cultural movement in film.

Until Lee's success, African American directors and motion-picture performers had a difficult road to travel. Their talent and vision were often compromised by Hollywood's ignorance of black culture.

Lee understands the power that comes with his position. "I have access to millions and millions of people through my films," he says. "Film invests me with a lot of power. The topics I choose to tackle in my films make a lot of people uncomfortable. It's the way we make the films. We try to go after the truth. Film is one of the most powerful mediums that we have. Films influence the way people dress, paint, talk, and all that. White Hollywood doesn't want everybody to have access to this power. They [white Hollywood film executives] don't want anybody to have access to all this money. They want to keep it all to themselves."[4]

Lee's success, moreover, has come on his own terms. Celebrity has always been a staple of the movie business. Hollywood has produced plenty of African American stars, from Hattie McDaniel to Dorothy Dandridge to Danny Glover. But Lee doesn't buy into the star system. (His films, however, have propelled Wesley Snipes, John Turturro, Rosie Perez, Halle Berry, Martin Lawrence, Tisha Campbell, and others to stardom.) "I don't feel like a movie star," Lee says. "I still take the subway. I live in Brooklyn one block from where I grew up. I don't have any bodyguards. I don't drive. I'm just grateful that I'm able to do what I love best, make films. A lot of people spend their entire lives doing a job they hate. When I pray every night, I thank God that I am able to do what I love. I am blessed."[5] Lee leaves the studio. The jungle awaits him. Broadway swelters. Lee surveys the scene on the street. He adjusts his baseball cap. He begins to walk down the Great White Way, and within a block he disappears through the heat waves into the subway.

FILMMAKER
SPIKE LEE.

ONE
Not a Pretty Picture

To appreciate the progression from the earliest African American performers and stars to Spike Lee and his contemporaries, it is necessary to consider film's relationship to society. Film has always been a good gauge of where a society stands. With its potential to create fantasy and rewrite reality, film shows what a society embraces and what it rejects.

The motion-picture industry began in the United States in the late 1800s. During these formative years, American society was in transition. The last shot in the Civil War had been fired less than fifty years before the first commercial films were made. Still bitter with the outcome of the Civil War, many southern whites had rebelled against Reconstruction, a federal program that sought to install governments loyal to the nation and integrate some four million newly freed slaves into American society. The notion that blacks were second-class people, even less than human, prevailed in the minds of many white Americans in the North and in the South.

he earliest films, which were silent, reflected these views. Made exclusively by white men, these movies contained unflattering depictions of African Americans. On the screen black Americans, portrayed by white actors in "black face" (coal-colored makeup derived from burnt cork), were represented as shiftless, dimwitted "darkies."

In 1903 a stooped, head-scratching, sweet old man appeared in the title role of a twelve-minute film, *Uncle Tom's Cabin*. The film was based on the controversial novel by Harriet Beecher Stowe. Many historians say that *Uncle Tom's Cabin* inspired the abolitionist movement in the North. Others point out that the book—and the movie—depicted grown blacks as children. The movie's Uncle Tom was played by a white man in black face. It was an instant smash.

Uncle Tom became one of white America's favorite movie characters. He would resurface as a stereotype time and again in films. He might be called Uncle Willie, Uncle Joe, or Uncle Pete in movies like *For Massa's Sake, Ten Pickaninnies*, or *The Wooing and Wedding of a Coon*. But he was always a sweet, gentle, simpleminded old man.

Then a female version of the Uncle Tom type appeared—as Mammy or Auntie. She wore a bandanna and waddled from side to side when she walked. She was fat. She cooked. She cleaned. She chased cowering black men with cast-iron skillets. She was fearless, except in her superstitions. She loved nothing more in the world than to take care of "white folk."

Joining these stereotypes was a cast of decidedly shadier black character types. There was the shuffling, shifty hooligan, usually named Rufus or Rastus. His sole function in life was to steal chickens and devour watermelons. Other blacks were depicted as brutes who terrorized whites, especially virtuous white women.

Some blacks (or, correctly, white actors in black face) possessed amazing musical skills. They played the scrub board and harmonica. They were "tap

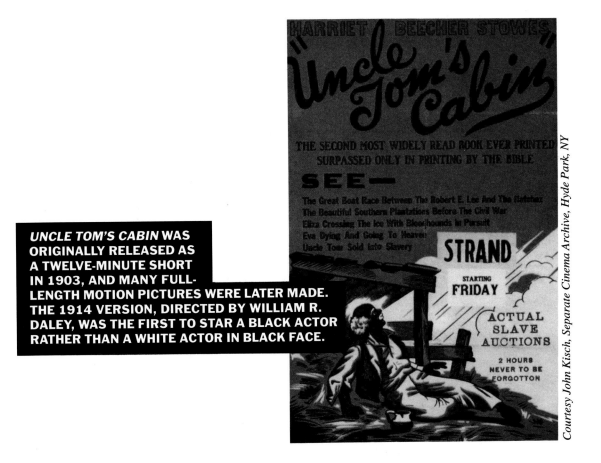

UNCLE TOM'S CABIN WAS ORIGINALLY RELEASED AS A TWELVE-MINUTE SHORT IN 1903, AND MANY FULL-LENGTH MOTION PICTURES WERE LATER MADE. THE 1914 VERSION, DIRECTED BY WILLIAM R. DALEY, WAS THE FIRST TO STAR A BLACK ACTOR RATHER THAN A WHITE ACTOR IN BLACK FACE.

Courtesy John Kisch, Separate Cinema Archive, Hyde Park, NY

dancing fools." The titles of popular films of the early 1900s reveal much about the filmmakers' attitudes toward blacks. *Interrupted Crap Game, Old Mammy's Secret Code, Chicken Thieves, How Rastus Got His Turkey,* and *Prize Fight in Coon Town* were all popular film shorts.

Such early films established a tradition of entertaining audiences at the expense of black Americans. By the time sound films or "talkies" arrived in the mid 1920s, black actors would play these roles. By far the most popular was Stepin Fetchit, the ultimate "trifling darkie," played by Lincoln Perry. Perry became a millionaire and the first black film star in America.

Film historian Donald Bogle noted that the objective of early white film-makers was to entertain through the use of stereotypes. "Fun was poked at the American Negro by presenting him as either a nitwit or a childlike lackey." [1] These images did double duty. They reflected and reinforced racist ideas about blacks.

In the controversial documentary *Black History; Lost, Stolen or Strayed,* Bill Cosby examined the motives of the Hollywood machine that cranked out such falsehoods: "Most Hollywood films, even the early ones, weren't really nasty. Nobody was sitting around saying, 'Let's take care of the niggers.' What producers were doing was making money. And to make money they made pictures that white ticket buyers would enjoy. They showed Negroes the way most Americans like to think of them." [2]

THE FATHER OF AMERICAN ● CINEMA

In 1915 director David Wark Griffith's *The Birth of a Nation* sent shock waves through America. The film was D. W. Griffith's version of the Reconstruction Era. It represented the bitterness that many southern whites felt in the aftermath of the Civil War. *The Birth of a Nation* cemented ugly screen images of African Americans that would prevail for decades to come. The film teems with "darkies" (white actors in black face) who over-run the once genteel South. They seize the government. They rape, plunder, and pillage whatever remains of the Old South. It did not matter that such atrocities never happened.

Griffith based his film on Thomas Dixon's novel *The Clansman,* which set out to rewrite history. "My object is to teach the North what it has never known—the awful suffering of the white man during the Reconstruction period," Dixon said. "I believe that dreadful almighty God anointed the white man by their suffering to demonstrate to the world that the white man can and must be supreme." [3]

THE CONTROVERSIAL FILM *THE BIRTH OF A NATION*, RELEASED IN 1915, WAS PRAISED BY PRESIDENT WOODROW WILSON AND MEMBERS OF CONGRESS, BUT CONDEMNED BY BLACK LEADERS AND CIVIL-RIGHTS ORGANIZATIONS.

Griffith had other powerful sources as well. He used the interpretation of Reconstruction presented in *History of the American People,* a book written by Woodrow Wilson while he was a professor of history at Princeton University. The future president of the United States wrote that blacks were "insolent and dangerous."[+]

The works of Dixon and Wilson were reflected in the film's twisting of history. Deliverance comes at last for suffering whites with the rise of the Ku Klux Klan. The horse-riding men in white sheets brandish burning crosses and exact terrible revenge on black people. Their noble aim is to restore the glory that was once the South.

Griffith shrewdly took advantage of America's barely healed wounds. He timed the film's release to coincide with the fiftieth anniversary of the Civil War. Technically, *The Birth of a Nation* was a masterpiece. More than two hours long, it was the longest film that had ever been released in America up to that time. Techniques never seen before, such as close-ups and cutaways, made the film extraordinarily powerful. Whites jammed theaters across the country to behold this epic. Special twenty-four-hour screenings were held to accommodate the crowds.

But many African Americans, particularly leaders such as W. E. B. Du Bois and Booker T. Washington were outraged by what they considered a brazen, bodacious, and barefaced lie. They felt that Griffith was exploiting an influential new technology to rewrite history.

During the Reconstruction Era, African Americans had made tremendous progress. They had to start from ground zero. Whatever the material and emotional losses that whites had suffered from the Civil War, they still enjoyed the privileges granted by their skin color. Blacks did not have this advantage. Nonetheless, in 1865 the Freedmen's Bureau, a federal agency, established educational services for newly emancipated southern blacks. Between 1865 and 1890 a number of black colleges were founded: Spelman, Tuskegee Institute, Fisk University, Morehouse, Howard University, and Hampton Institute among them. These institutions were supported by religious orders and the foundations of wealthy white businessmen. These colleges produced thousands of black tradesmen and professionals. (More than one hundred years after its founding, Morehouse College would graduate Spike Lee.)

The National Association for the Advancement of Colored People (NAACP), which was founded in 1909, launched a nationwide protest against *The Birth of a Nation*. The young civil-rights organization, which comprised blacks and their liberal Jewish supporters, was not powerful enough to stop distribution of the film. The NAACP did manage, however, to have *The Birth of a Nation* banned in Chicago, Cleveland, and St. Louis, all cities with large black populations. The NAACP also succeeded in having several scenes cut from the movie. Among the most grisly was a mob scene in which a black (a white actor in black face) was lynched and castrated. Throughout 1915, W. E. B. Du Bois, the editor of *Crisis*, the magazine of the NAACP, would blast the film in editorial after editorial. Du Bois was the first black graduate to receive a doctorate degree at Harvard University. He was an intellectual heavyweight in twentieth-century America as well as an international presence.

His earliest criticism was directed at author Thomas Dixon: "Small wonder that a man who can thus brutally falsify history has never been able to do a single piece of literary work that has brought the slightest attention except when he seeks to capitalize burning race antagonisms."[5]

The October issue of *Crisis* noted: "While the NAACP has failed to kill *The Birth of a Nation* it has at least succeeded in wounding it." The issue also reserved strong words for Griffith: "We trust that such an artistic producer as Mr. Griffith may never again make the mistake of choosing an iniquitous story as a medium for his genius, or as a quick method of accumulating a fortune."[6]

There was at least one African American for whom the film represented bitter personal disappointment. Her name was Cora. She was D. W. Griffith's beloved maid. On the night of the premiere Griffith arranged for Cora to sit in a choice seat in a segregated theater. Attired in her Sunday finery, Cora felt

honored to attend the gala. Midway through the film she stormed out. The next day she gave Griffith a piece of her mind. "Mr. Griffith, I am ashamed of you," she said. "I am ashamed of the way you treated my people. I named my son after you and I am changing that name today. Good-bye."[7]

Cora's reaction was definitely a minority opinion. A special screening was held for the U.S. Congress. The lawmakers gave it a standing ovation. President Wilson, a graduate-school classmate of Griffith's, a historian, former president of Princeton University, and native of Virginia, was charmed by the film. "It's like writing history with lightning," he said. His "only regret" about the film was that it was "all so terribly true."[8]

Eighty years after the film's release, the debate still raged. At a 1994 symposium held at the Smithsonian Institution in Washington, D.C., leading scholars met to evaluate the film's impact on American society. Historian John Hope Franklin felt that the film had poisoned the minds of white America. "The lesson that this film taught over and over again…was that it was a tragic mistake to have given African Americans the vote in the era of Reconstruction. In the years following World War I, Klansmen assumed the responsibility of keeping alive the lessons of *The Birth of a Nation*."[9]

Emmett J. Scott, an assistant to Booker T. Washington, the president of Tuskegee University, began working on a film called *The Birth of a Race*. Intended as a response to Griffith's work, it was released in 1918, three years after Washington's death. According to film historians, both black and white, the three-hour film was a technical disaster.

RACE FILMS

a few years before the United States entered World War I in 1917 the first Great Migration of African Americans began. Blacks left the rural South to work in northern factories. The new urban populations entertained themselves differently from the way they did "down home." The traditional southern Saturday night fish fry or sweaty evening dance in a crowded "juke joint" was replaced in the cities with more sophisticated pastimes. Race music, controlled by white-owned record companies, did big business with artists like Bessie Smith (the Queen of the Blues) and ragtime pianist Jelly Roll Morton. Negro League baseball was barnstorming the country, making celebrities out of athletes like Satchel Paige, Josh Gibson, and "Cool Papa" Bell. (In the 1970s, Motown, the successful black-owned music company, produced *The Bingo Long Traveling All-Stars and Motor Kings*, a comedy about life in the Negro Leagues.)

In this climate of cultural progress, black entrepreneurs tried their hand at filmmaking, using their own money or entering into partnerships with whites. The Lincoln Film Company, the Frederick Douglass Company, and the Micheaux Company produced movies about black life that were shown in theaters, churches, apartments, schools, and at meetings and conventions of Black Greek fraternities and sororities. The motto of the Lincoln Film Company, headquartered in Chicago, was "to picture the Negro as he is in everyday life."[10] Films like *The Homesteader, Murder in Harlem*, and *The Girl From Chicago* were produced far away from what had now become glittering Hollywood. They were made on shoestring budgets and shown at "colored only" theaters. These films were known as race movies.

During the 1920s, 30s, and 40s, Jim Crow segregation prevented blacks and whites from patronizing the same theaters. And in that respect segregation actually represented a blessing for the early black filmmakers. Segregation created a market for black film. About 150 companies emerged that specialized in race movies. About fifty of these were black-owned.

Race movies were a welcome relief from the degrading images of blacks that white filmmakers created. "Race movies were important to black audiences because [they] provided them with images of themselves that they didn't see in regular cinema," said film historian Pearl Bowser.[11] The race movies generally presented blacks as professionals and well-to-do people. The characters dressed in sharp business suits and elegant evening gowns. The men were handsome, and the women were stunning. These images were a far cry from the bug-eyed Uncle Tom and the big waddling Mammy.

THE FATHER OF AFRICAN AMERICAN CINEMA

t he most successful independent black filmmaker of the time was Oscar Micheaux, a man of immense determination. A novelist, farmer, and railroad porter from South Dakota, Micheaux was a jack-of-all-trades. Between 1919 and 1948 he produced more than thirty films.

Money was always tight for Micheaux. Relentlessly he raised funds to finance his productions. Unlike top white filmmakers who usually had huge amounts of cash at their disposal, Micheaux had to make every penny count. He could not afford to pay his cast and crew top dollar. Usually he shot his films in one take. The standard practice of shooting a scene several times and editing the best takes was out of the question. Flubbed lines and miscues stayed.

Micheaux took white stories and gave them a cinematic suntan. His movies were filled with cowboys, chorus girls, gangsters, and women in distress—all stock, or common, Hollywood characters. In one sense Micheaux took these elements and tailored them to his own needs and to what he saw as the needs of his audience. When Lorenzo Tucker, one of his leading men, questioned the director on his use of elaborate dance numbers that seemed out of place in some of his pictures, Micheaux told him that movies should allow people to escape mundane reality. "There's excitement in seeing a colored cast that is not picking cotton. The pretty girls are for the poor guys down South who want to see some pretty legs, dancing, and beautiful girls."[12]

Micheaux's work reflected the extent to which slavery had damaged the psyche of African Americans. Color prejudice within the black community was (and remains) a sensitive issue that dated from the plantation. European standards of beauty were very evident in Micheaux's work. In most of his films the stars were light-skinned blacks, many of whom resembled popular white stars of the day. Guess who got to play the role of the wayward Negroes? The dark-skinned actors, the "dusky" actors, as they were called in those days. Micheaux billed heartthrobs like Lorenzo Tucker, "the black Valentino." Singer

Herb Jeffrey, the tall and dashing hero of several early black westerns, was called "the black Gene Autry." The biggest star of Micheaux's films was Nina Mae McKinney. Light-skinned enough to "pass" for white, she usually played the tragic mulatto whose life was hell. Her characters occupied the uncomfortable world between black and white. She became America's first black female sex symbol. Actresses like Fredi Washington, Lena Horne, Dorothy Dandridge, Lonette McKee, Jada Pinkett, and Halle Berry, who bore similar physical features, would follow in her path.

Although he was an independent, Micheaux had style—Hollywood style. He traveled the country in a chauffeur-driven limousine promoting his films. Without the backing of a major studio, he was a one-man operation. He convinced churches and black businesses to invest in his films. He also struck deals with the owners of "colored" theaters in the South. Many of these owners were black. They knew that Micheaux's films made money. Micheaux even convinced the owners of whites-only theaters to hold late-night screenings of his movies. These sessions, which usually ran from midnight to 2:00 A.M., were billed as "midnight rambles." The only sign of strain that showed itself on the hardworking Micheaux was a stomach disorder. Whenever Micheaux was shooting a film, he had to lie on a couch and eat handfuls of cornstarch.

Black audiences savored films like Micheaux's *Body and Soul,* a 1925 silent film about a wayward preacher, which was the debut of actor Paul Robeson. Bee Freeman, an actress who appeared in many of Micheaux's movies, pointed out, "All of Mr. Micheaux's pictures should be looked upon as a beginning. They were a stepping stone to better things." [13]

Spencer Williams was another popular director. *Dirty Gertie From Harlem, U.S.A.* is one of his most popular works. Like Micheaux's films, his work provided alternative images for black moviegoers. After the bombardment of earlier movies and their degrading depictions, race movies were a godsend. "One of the things that race films answered was the echo [for a new image of black immigrants from "down home"]. 'I want to hear myself. I want to see myself,'" writer Toni Cade Bambara said. [14]

BLACK AND TAN STARS IN HOLLYWOOD

hollywood movie studios, having observed Micheaux's success, began producing all-black feature films. The most successful films produced by big-time studios were the "all colored" musicals. These films showcased the awesome talents of dancers like the Nicholas Brothers and Sammy Davis, Jr. At the same time, studios refused to abandon degrading images of blacks. Master tap dancer Bill "Bojangles" Robinson played the caretaker for Shirley Temple, the dimpled darling of *Rebecca of Sunnybrook Farm* and *The Littlest Rebel.* Films like the Christian melodrama *The Green Pastures* featured dark-skinned, bushy-headed "chillun" (children) playing the harp and lazing on the clouds of "heben" (heaven).

TAP DANCER BILL "BOJANGLES" ROBINSON
WITH SHIRLEY TEMPLE IN *THE LITTLE COLONEL* (1935).

Many movies that featured white casts included musical segments of black artists like Billie Holiday, Louis Armstrong, and Lena Horne. Usually they were in a nightclub scene entertaining white patrons. Not everyone found their performances entertaining. "Integration," even at this level, was still too disturbing for some white censors in the segregated South. These segments were cut from prints sent to southern theaters.

One of the day's most spectacular musicals was *Hallelujah*. King Vidor was the director. Of his "secret hope" to direct all-black films, Vidor, who is white, wrote, "I wanted to make a film about Negroes using only Negroes in the cast. The sincerity and fervor of their religious expression intrigued me, as did the honest simplicity of their sexual drives." [15]

1929 POSTER FOR *HALLELUJAH*, DIRECTED BY KING VIDOR, THE SECOND MUSICAL TO HAVE AN ALL-BLACK CAST. *HEARTS IN DIXIE* WAS THE FIRST, RELEASED THAT SAME YEAR.

although such stereotypes were blatantly racist, some black actors became millionaires playing them. Foremost among them was Stepin Fetchit. Named after four American presidents, Lincoln Theodore Monroe Andrew Perry was born in Florida around the turn of the century. He became Hollywood's first black star. One critic called him "a walking windup toy for the amusement of whites." [16] As a comedic actor Perry specialized in playing a mumbling, slow-talking servant. His popular films included *Hearts in Dixie, The Galloping Ghost, Swing High,* and *Helldorado.* He often shared top billing with whites. There was never a problem with southern censors refusing to show Perry's films. They loved him. His career spanned more than forty films.

Many blacks of the day were disgusted by Stepin Fetchit. But Perry defended his work as art. And indeed it was that to many. He enjoyed the respect of Charlie Chaplin, Buster Keaton, and other film greats from the silent movie era. His work in talkies would influence comedic actors like Jerry Lewis and Dean Martin. Describing his approach to the *New York Evening Post,* he said, "I call it audible pantomiming. It's a new art, born with talking pictures. I made my start in Hollywood on the silent screen when pantomime was all-important. When speech came along, film comics were up against a new program—to fit their funny gestures to words, or to fit the words to gestures, however you look at it."

Perry was certainly one of the few silent screen actors to successfully cross over to the talkies. "I decided to go ahead pantomiming just as I'd always done. I picked out the important words in the lines I had, the ones important for laughs, or that gave cues to other actors; I consciously stressed them—the rest of the speech doesn't matter. I mumble through the rest, gestures helping to paint the situation." [17] "We have not extolled the virtues of Lincoln Perry's art," declared film critic Clayton Riley. "The clown is an honored traditon in many societies. Jerry Lewis is a prince in his tribe. Lincoln Perry was not.

LINCOLN THEODORE MONROE ANDREW PERRY,

What he did was great art outside of the context of what it meant to the race in political terms. Tell me the difference between a Tom performed well and a Tom performed amateurishly. Most people don't bother to look at the difference." [18]

Perry ignored his critics and flaunted his wealth. He was a peacock on parade. During his heyday Perry resided in an exclusive "colored" section of Los Angeles, employing sixteen Chinese servants (an ethnic status symbol of the day for the wealthy). He owned twelve cars, among them a pink Rolls Royce. On the back of each automobile was an electric sign bearing his name. Each car came with its own set of chauffeurs—one for each hour of the day. He lived the fast Hollywood life. He squandered millions. He drank. He partied. He engaged in street brawls. He was charged with paternity suits. His escapades were reported in newspapers and gossip magazines from coast to coast.

Directors often let Perry set up his own scenes. He stressed that he would not be manipulated. He considered his work a high form of cinematic acting. "I don't care who the director is—if he isn't colored, he hasn't got that feeling which comes from the Negro soul. It's up to him to allow the colored actor some liberty when he's playing a part. There never has been a picture yet with colored players which hasn't lacked the natural interpretation of the Negro."

But he also professed dreams beyond the role of Stepin Fetchit. "I have written a true Negro script called *Skeeter,* which I hope some day to be permitted to direct. I don't want to boss the whole picture—just direct the colored players—and I'll show you something that's never been done before." [19] That plan remained nothing but a wish. When Perry finally set up a production company to film the lives of Jack Johnson, the controversial world heavyweight boxing champion, and Satchel Paige, the baseball great, his efforts went nowhere.

"Stepin Fetchit became a millionaire by playing the world's laziest man," observed director Matt Robinson, who directed Perry in 1974 in *Amazing*

Grace. "But he never changed his act. He was basically the same character in all of his films. Progressive black people had a problem with that. With growing prosperity and the civil rights movement, blacks became bolder. Society changed, but Stepin Fetchit didn't. He became out of joint with the times." [20]

In the years before his death in 1985, Perry was a bitter man. He felt that no one appreciated his artistic skills. "When I came into motion pictures, it was as an individual. I had no manager, and no one had the idea of making a Negro a star. I became the first Negro entertainer to become a millionaire. All the things that Bill Cosby and Sidney Poitier have done wouldn't be possible if I hadn't broken the law. I set up thrones for them to come and sit on." [21]

EMPEROR ROBESON

many great black actors such as Nina Mae McKinney and Clarence Muse grew frustrated with the limited options that Hollywood presented them. Probably no career was more tragically circumscribed than that of Paul Robeson. The six-foot-three-inch Robeson was the epitome of what Du Bois termed "the talented tenth." Du Bois believed that a tenth of the African American population, through academic excellence, could lead the rest of the race to full citizenship in the United States. Robeson certainly fit the bill. He was nothing short of phenomenal.

The son of a former slave, Robeson was born in 1898. A Phi Beta Kappa honors graduate of Rutgers University, he was an All-American defensive end and track star. He received his doctor of law degree from Columbia Law School. Yet Robeson's awesome academic and athletic talents paled in comparison to his musical and dramatic abilities. Robeson possessed a thunderous singing voice. His portrayal of Othello on Broadway was considered by many to have been among the best. The production holds the record for the longest-running Shakespearean play on Broadway. Moreover, Robeson was the first black actor to appear in the role of the Moor in America. The history he was making was not lost on Robeson. "Here is a part that has dignity for the Negro actor," he told an interviewer. "Often we don't get those opportunities. My people will be very proud of my, or any other Negro actor, appearing in such a part." [22]

Statuesque and ruggedly handsome, Robeson was a forceful presence on the stage, on screen, and in concert halls. His intellect and pride would not allow him to play demeaning roles. Despite his good looks, he refused to be cast as a sex symbol. Robeson was also outspoken about racism and politics in America. Unlike most film actors, black or white, he did not hold his tongue.

His greatest role was in a film version of Eugene O'Neill's *The Emperor Jones* in 1933. Robeson portrayed Brutus Jones, a Pullman porter who flees the country for an island after murdering a friend in a crap game. He contrives to overthrow the king and name himself emperor. He rules with an iron hand until the inhabitants put a voodoo hex on him and he's haunted by the spirit of the man he murdered. With drums pounding in the background, a symbol of his conscience, his subjects stalk him through the jungle and kill him.

The Emperor Jones presented America with an image of a black man that they had never seen before. Robeson's Jones was smart, regal, and cunning. He was no foolish Tom. Robeson's only misgiving about *The Emperor Jones* was that it cast a black man as a murderer.

Historian Donald Bogle pointed out how radical the character of Brutus Jones was: "Surely, as Robeson was seen standing by this throne with a crown on his head and a scepter in his hand, as he ordered his old white partner about, black audiences must have felt immensely proud and fond of that bad nigger up there on the screen, telling them white folks to get outta his way to give him room to breathe." [23]

In his personal life Robeson demonstrated his intellect. He spoke out against discrimination. He supported organized labor. He supported the People's Republic of China, then a newly formed Communist state. Many film historians have concluded that Robeson's mind and masculinity were too much for white America to handle. Eventually, because of his political beliefs, Robeson was blackballed from the film industry. In 1950 the State

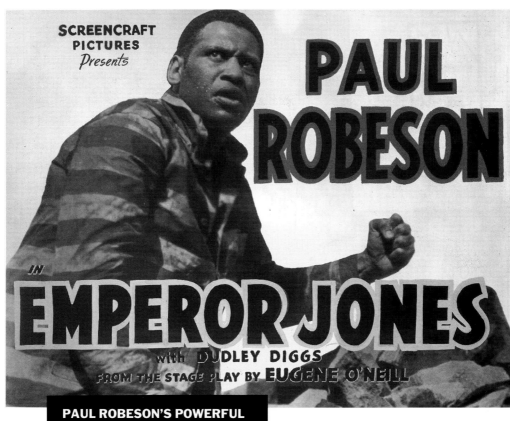

SCREENCRAFT
PICTURES
Presents

PAUL
ROBESON

in
EMPEROR JONES

with DUDLEY DIGGS
FROM THE STAGE PLAY BY EUGENE O'NEILL

**PAUL ROBESON'S POWERFUL
DEPICTION OF BRUTUS JONES
WAS A MARKED CONTRAST TO THE PREVIOUS
ROLES PLAYED BY BLACK ACTORS.**

Department revoked his passport. An official statement read: "This action is taken because the department considers that Paul Robeson's travel abroad would be contrary to the best interests of the United States."[24] The move crippled his career and robbed Robeson of his health. He fought back. Eight years later the Supreme Court ruled that the State Department had no constitutional basis for seizing his passport. "Here's a question of whether one wants to sing and act and have a political opinion," Robeson responded. "[State

Department officials] suggested that when I was abroad I spoke out against segregation in the United States. I certainly did."[25]

Writer James Baldwin was among the millions of Americans who believed that Robeson was handed a raw deal. Baldwin bitterly argued that America short-changed Robeson, who was undoubtedly one of the greatest artists that the country had ever produced. "It is scarcely possible to think of a black American actor who has not been misused," Baldwin noted. "Not one has ever been seriously challenged to deliver the best that is in him. The most powerful examples of this cowardice and waste are the careers of Paul Robeson and Ethel Waters. If they had ever been allowed to really hit their stride, they might have raised immeasurably the level of cinema and theater in this country."[26]

MAMMY

another brilliant actor caught in the catch-22 of Hollywood's early portrayals of blacks was Hattie McDaniel. McDaniel is best remembered for her role in the 1939 classic *Gone With the Wind*. Set in a highly romanticized version of the American South during the Civil War and Reconstruction, the film tells the story of Rhett Butler and Scarlett O'Hara, two headstrong southerners. Always at Miss Scarlett's side is her maid, Mammy, played by McDaniel.

Based on a best-selling novel, the film promised to be a blockbuster. Competition for the role of Mammy was tough. Louise Beavers, the other reigning Mammy of the silver screen, read for the part. President and Mrs. Roosevelt sent their personal maid, Elizabeth McDuffie (also known as Mammy Whitehouse) to audition for the part. Hattie McDaniel won the role. With her performance McDaniel would solidify Mammy's place in film history. She waddles, fusses, and rolls her eyes throughout the movie. When Mammy is on the screen, everybody knows it. She is a scene stealer.

For this performance, McDaniel became the first African American to win an Oscar. Millions of Americans heard her acceptance speech on radio and saw her on newsreels. She thanked those who had awarded her "for

HATTIE McDANIEL, VIVIAN LEIGH,
AND CARROLL NYE IN THE 1939
CLASSIC *GONE WITH THE WIND*, DIRECTED BY VICTOR FLEMING.

your kindness. It has made me feel very, very humble and I shall always hold it as a beacon for anything that I may be able to do in the future. I sincerely hope I shall always be a credit to my race and to the motion-picture industry...."[27]

Before she could wipe the tears of joy from her eyes, McDaniel was slighted. At an exclusive celebration at the Coconut Grove nightclub in Los Angeles, McDaniel and her escort, a black actor named Wonderful Jones, were snubbed. They were seated in a remote corner of the club. A sobbing McDaniel, resplendent in gardenias, purple evening dress, and fur coat, was comforted by her producer, David O. Selznick.[28] America loved McDaniel, but even as an African American movie star she was not exempt from racism. When she moved onto Country Club Drive, an exclusive address in the white section of Hollywood, the award-winning actress was greeted with burning crosses on her lawn, the calling card of the Ku Klux Klan.

Like Stepin Fetchit, McDaniel met strong protest from black groups. Walter White, assistant executive secretary of the NAACP, was among her strongest critics. He launched a one-man crusade to curtail the careers of people like Perry and McDaniel. He pressed studio executives to make films that showed blacks in a more positive light. His black actors of choice to star in such films were people like Lena Horne. White himself was a light-skinned black who could easily "pass" if he so desired. Upon meeting people for the first time, White was fond of laying his race card on the table. "I am a Negro. My skin is white. My eyes are blue. My hair is blonde. The traits of my race are nowhere visible upon me."[29]

Many black actors saw White as a phony. He attacked them. They counterattacked. McDaniel was not one to back down. She had paid a lot of dues to get where she was. She often estimated that she had washed about three million dishes before she became a full-time actress. Moreover, she was one of the more civic-minded members of the Hollywood community. "I'd rather play a maid than be one," she snapped. "Why should I complain about making seven thousand dollars a week playing a maid? If I didn't I'd be making seven dollars a week actually being one!"[30]

Throughout her career, which would span more than eighty films, McDaniel was a servant with sass. In *Gone With the Wind*, Mammy stares her white employers dead in the eye and talks back. She advises Miss Scarlett to "stop acting like po' white trash." Such back talk was unheard of in real life. McDaniel accused her detractors of behaving like crabs in a barrel. "I've never heard a single white person say one bad word about me. All your own censors seem to be among your own people."[31]

Were her critics (namely Walter White) wrong to dismiss her work as rubbish? That question remains debatable, but McDaniel gave memorable performances. "This is an extraordinary history that is so rich in its complexities," Clayton Riley noted of McDaniel and her career. "She was a woman of such commanding presence that photographs of her, beyond the studio photographs, revealed the sort of face that you would see in African mask art. That's how exceptionally fine this woman's features were. We just think of her as wearing a rag around her head. She really was a fine dramatic actress."[32]

The tragedy of McDaniel was that she was doomed to play Mammy roles for the rest of her career. She was allowed to drop the "dese and dem" dialect that was scripted for most Hollywood servants, but as an actress she had no real power. She even suggested that the NAACP produce and direct films. "What do you want me to do? Play a glamour girl and sit on Clark Gable's knee? [This would have been quite an accomplishment considering that the actress wore a size 44 dress and weighed nearly 300 pounds.] When you ask me not to play the part, what have you got to offer in return?"[33]

In order to maintain her stardom McDaniel had to maintain a bulky size. Like many African Americans, McDaniel suffered from high blood pressure. Her weight did not help. She quietly battled cancer for the last decade of her life. When she died of complications from a stroke in 1952, the film industry gave her a star's sendoff. Three thousand mourners paid their final respects. The funeral cortege included twenty-four limousines and three hearses. One hearse carried McDaniel to her final resting place. The other two were laden with flowers. Mammy was dead.

TWO

The Dark Screen

Hollywood's recognition that black actors could draw audiences signaled the death of race films. Oscar Micheaux, the last of the independent filmmakers, closed up shop in 1948. Few followed in his footsteps. More blacks pursued careers as Hollywood actors. Among the handful of filmmakers, a young actor named William Greaves made worthwhile documentaries and newsreels. *All-American News,* produced by William D. Alexander and Claude A. Barnett, also provided a truthful and intelligent look at black life and accomplishments.

To many blacks at the time—and in retrospect—these newsreels appeared more truthful than those produced by white companies. With the exception of those focusing on "super Negroes" like Ralph Bunche, the United Nations diplomat, or Jackie Robinson, the first Negro to play in the major leagues, some newsreels produced by whites distorted black life and perpetuated demeaning stereotypes. One short, *Watermelon Derby,* showed dozens of black men thrusting their faces into watermelon. The text on the screen read: "Darkies down in Waterville, Mississippi, get up to their ears in eating race." [1]

Meanwhile new actors emerged. Among them were Diahann Carroll, Pearl Bailey, Sammy Davis, Jr., Harry Belafonte, Ruby Dee, Ossie Davis, Eartha Kitt, and the sexy and tragic Dorothy Dandridge. Many of these actors began their careers with black theater groups. Under white directors and Hollywood studios, these actors starred in some fine films. Among them were *St. Louis Blues*, *Pinky*, and *Porgy and Bess*, based on the George Gershwin opera.

SIDNEY POITIER: THE NEW NEGRO

Sidney Poitier, star of *Porgy and Bess*, was the black man who would defy stereotypical roles and emerge as the first dramatic screen artist who was not shuffling and taking care of "white folk."

Poitier was born in Miami in 1927 and grew up on Cat Island in the Bahamas. His family was poor. In search of a job, he returned to the United States during the 1940s. As he searched for work, first in Miami then in New York, he happened upon a small classified advertisement for stage actors. The audition was held by a small repertory company, the American Negro Theater. Poitier was ready to try anything. "I knew nothing about theater," Poitier recalled in his autobiography. "Nothing about acting, knew no actors or actresses except those I had seen in movies and that was different: first of all they were white."[2]

Poitier auditioned for Frederick O'Neal, director of Harlem's prestigious American Negro Theater and a noted stage actor. Poitier was dismal. In fact, he recalls that O'Neal literally threw him out the door.

Poitier took the rejection as a challenge. A spark caught, and he studied acting relentlessly. Every day he listened to the radio and imitated American dialects and syntax. He was determined to reserve his Caribbean speaking voice for family and friends. Eventually his hard work paid off. Upon his return to the American Negro Theater six months later, Poitier won a spot in the company. He took roles in off-Broadway productions. By the time he appeared in *Anna Lucasta* on Broadway, Poitier's star was rising—and fast.

Poitier soon moved to film. He starred in a series of dramas: *Cry; The Beloved Country, A Patch of Blue, A Raisin in the Sun, Lilies of the Field, Black Board Jungle, The Defiant Ones,* and more. Often he was co-billed with white actors, such as Shelley Winters, Katharine Hepburn, Rod Steiger, or Tony Curtis. Poitier usually played a lone, educated, or highly skilled black man who walks into an all-white situation. He is in command and charming. At some point in each of these movies the whites are forced to confront their prejudice. Throughout Poitier barely smiles, rarely dances, and almost always displays cool restraint and quick comebacks in the face of insults.

Poitier was a Hollywood creation, but also a creature of the times. "The Civil Rights Movement was in full swing," director Matt Robinson pointed out. "After years of Mammy and Stepin Fetchit, and messing over talented actors like Paul Robeson, Hollywood had to come up with something. Sidney Poitier was the right man for the right times." [3]

Beyond the political and social changes sweeping America was the fact that Poitier was a great actor. Physically he could not be ignored. Poitier stood 6 feet 2 inches, and his dark skin had the sheen of a Bahamian night. His facial features were keen and piercing. During the era of black-and-white movies, Poitier contrasted starkly with his white co-stars. Eyes remained riveted on Poitier when he was on the screen. "To understand art as an extension of human beauty, you have to be able to see this man in full performance," Clayton Riley observed. "Poitier was very successful in his body art. You could do a whole evening of just watching Poitier's walk or Poitier pointing out something, Poitier turning. He was very specific about these kinds of things. He understood what the camera was doing when he was working. He understood that movies asked for very vivid and specific stylizations. He had the physical movements. He had the grace." [4]

Perhaps one of his most complex stage and film roles was that of Walter Lee Younger, the father of a working-class family on the South Side of Chicago in *A Raisin in the Sun.* The play appeared on the big screen in 1961. Written by Lorraine Hansberry, a young African American playwright, *A Raisin In the*

Sun won the New York Drama Critics Circle Award in 1959. The title was inspired by a line in the poem "Harlem" by Langston Hughes:

What happens to a dream deferred?
Does it dry up
like a raisin in the sun? [5]

As Walter Lee Younger, Poitier is torn over how to best use the $10,000 his mother has collected from his dead father's insurance policy. Should he move his family into a hostile suburb or invest money in a liquor store with two shady friends, Bobo and Willy. Poitier plays the part of a divided soul with searing intensity.

The best was yet to come.

In the 1963 film *Lilies of the Field,* he portrayed Homer Smith, an ex-G.I. and wandering handyman who befriends a group of German immigrant nuns in the middle of the Arizona desert. Homer Smith is their dark angel. "God is good," the Mother Superior proclaims when she first meets Homer. "He has sent me a big, strong man." The nuns cajole Homer into building a chapel for them. (Homer tells them that he is not even Catholic. He's a black Baptist.) Homer is a good-natured guy. He teaches the nuns English. He buys them groceries, or "real food," as he calls it. (Homer likes grits, potatoes, bacon, eggs, and pancakes for breakfast. By contrast, the nuns eat "bird food.") In short order he is using the Bible to argue with the penny-pinching mother superior over his wages. She pulls out a German version of the Good Book and finds a passage of scripture that says he should give freely to God. Homer and the Mother Superior go tit for tat. (Ultimately, she wins. The nuns get Homer's labor for free.)

This character was the opposite of Walter Lee Younger. The film's theme song was a rendition of "Amen," the standard Christian hymn. One year after the film was released, it was performed in simple three-part harmony by the Impressions, a popular rhythm and blues trio. (Nearly twenty years later, Curtis

SIDNEY POITIER WAS THE FIRST
BLACK ACTOR TO WIN AN ACADEMY
AWARD, WHICH HE RECEIVED FOR HIS ROLE AS HOMER SMITH IN
THE 1963 FILM *LILIES OF THE FIELD*, DIRECTED BY RALPH NELSON.

Mayfield, the founder and lead singer of the group, would compose the music for the controversial "blaxploitation" classic *Superfly.)*

Homer Smith, the nice guy, finished first at the Oscars. Poitier won the Academy Award for Best Actor in 1963. He was the first African American male to do so. (Louis Gossett, Jr., and Denzel Washington would follow with awards for Best Supporting Actor for their respective performances in *An Officer and a Gentleman* in 1982 and *Glory* in 1989.) As Best Actor, Poitier was at the top of the film industry. Even Hattie McDaniel had only achieved Best Supporting Actress. It was a long road from Mammy to Homer Smith. When his name was announced as the winner, Poitier abandoned his trademark reserve and leaped into the air. A few moments later, a more collected Poitier stepped up to the podium to collect the coveted gold statue. He acknowledged both his personal history and that of his race. Sighing, he told the audience at the Santa Monica Civic Auditorium, "It's been a long journey to this moment."[6] Poitier wore a white bow tie and black tails and a beaming smile.

The next day Poitier discussed with the *New York Times* the impact his victory would have for blacks in films. "I like to think that it will help someone. But I don't believe my Oscar will be a sort of magic wand that will wipe away the restrictions on job opportunities for Negro actors."[7]

But Poitier could not satisfy everyone. Some had to qualify his success. Of the ovation that followed his acceptance speech, one journalist noted: "The outburst. . .was recognition not only of his talent, but also of the fact that Hollywood has felt guilty about color barriers of the past, some of which still exist here."[8]

Many black militants were critical of the good-guy image that Poitier projected. They charged that he was a new, more polite, and well-groomed version of Uncle Tom. Their criticism was brutal. Phrases like "tar baby," "Hollywood bunny," and "million-dollar shoe shine boy," were used to describe Poitier and his work. For Hattie McDaniel these would have been fighting words. But Poitier played it cool. He refused to dignify such critics with a response. He realized that this was their way of building their own reputations. Years later Poitier said that he resented one critic in particular for "laying all of the film industry's transgressions at my feet."[9]

Despite his success, Poitier was mindful of the fact that he still had no real power in Tinseltown. He reflected in his autobiography, *This Life:*

Hollywood had not kept it secret that it wasn't interested in supplying blacks with a variety of positive images. In fact, in only a few isolated corners of the industry could one find committed souls who could be classified as interested in supplying blacks with a different image from what they had been accustomed to. Thanks to that handful of committed souls, the image of the black man just scratching his head was changing. A black man was put in a suit with a tie, given a briefcase; he could become a doctor, a lawyer, or a police detective. A people are a community, and a community consists of bus drivers and laborers and street sweepers and dentists and school teachers and hustlers and prostitutes and students and ordinary workers—people, people. They fall in love, they have problems, they have children, they live, they die. Where was that kind of representation on the motion picture screen for blacks? It didn't exist. The closest Hollywood came…was the one-dimensional middle class imagery I embodied most of the time. Although I considered it a step forward, it was not a step that could in any way alleviate all the frustrations of the past decades. The dilemma for me was that there was nothing I could do in quick relief for the guy who works in a factory, who's married to a good wife who doesn't look like Denise Nicholas or Dorothy Dandridge but who loves him and has given him a couple of fine kids with whom they have a very good black family home life, the likes of which he wants to see reflected on the motion picture screen when he plunks down his three or four dollars.

I couldn't do that for him because I was not in control of the film business. I was not even in control of my career in the film business beyond making a decision to play or not to play in a given piece of material.[10]

BLACK POWER

much of what Poitier was describing, however, was about to change. By the late 1960s, the Black Power Movement was in full force. It was characterized by radical thought and dress. Revolution, black pride, fiery poetry readings, huge afros, and colorful African print pattern shirts called dashikis were the order of the day. Politics were hot. Many young African Americans returned to the teachings of Marcus Garvey, who had founded the "back to Africa" movement, and the pan-Africanism of W. E. B. Du Bois. (Pan-Africanism is the belief that all people of African descent have common interests and should work together for common goals.) Frantz Fanon, a scholar from Martinique, was another often-quoted figure.

When Dr. Martin Luther King, Jr.'s nonviolent quest for Negro equality and respectability was ended by an assassin's bullets, militant young blacks like H. Rap Brown and Stokley Carmichael, and radical black organizations like the Congress for Racial Equality (CORE) and the Black Panthers challenged the American establishment and the traditional civil-rights movement over strategies for progress. They were tired of taking "stuff off the man." Many said they preferred not to deal with white people, period. Such a stance was contradictory. These militant organizations and their leaders frequently received support, including funding, from liberal whites, many of them in the entertainment industry. Composer Leonard Bernstein, actress Jane Fonda, and Otto Preminger, the director of *Carmen Jones* and *Porgy and Bess*, made generous contributions to the Black Power movement.

Away from the cocktail parties that brought black radicals and their white supporters together, life in urban America was far from a wine-and-cheese reception. Many poor people were trapped in the nation's large cities. Many middle-class whites had fled to the suburbs, taking their tax dollars with them. The cities were crumbling, and schools did not educate. Police brutality was an everyday thing in the ghetto. A policeman's billy club or an insult could set off an explosion. Riots erupted in the inner cities of Philadelphia, Los Angeles, Detroit, Chicago, St. Louis, and elsewhere.

These real-life dramas were not acted out by men resembling Sidney Poitier's image of the black man. It didn't matter that Poitier was the top box-office star of 1967. Many joked that in real life Homer Smith, the character Poitier played in *Lilies of the Field,* probably would have to go to the middle of the desert to find work. He certainly couldn't find work in his own neighborhood. A new character, one who walked the ghetto streets, was about to appear on the movie screen. He wasn't mister nice guy.

His name was Sweetback.

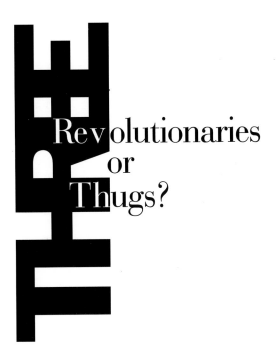

Revolutionaries or Thugs?

Sweetback was the hero of Melvin Van Peeble's 1971 film, *Sweet Sweetback's Baadasssss Song.* The film tells the hardcore tale of a black hustler from the Watts section of Los Angeles. It is the story of a fugitive. Sweetback kills two white police officers after they brutalize a young revolutionary named Moo Moo. Sweetback cannot turn his back on the scene and executes—as the film describes it—some "ghetto-style justice." But the "white man's justice" doesn't let him walk away. So he runs.

Sweetback runs (and runs and runs) for his life to the U.S.-Mexico border. From the film's perspective, this is the price a black man must pay when he dares to "kick some a—."

In one sense, Sweetback was totally different from any black character that had previously appeared on the screen. Whites had made films with menacing blacks, but this story is told from a black man's point of view. For the first time on film, a downtrodden black man fights back. He also runs, but throughout his flight Sweetback, "a brother from the streets," outsmarts racist whites.

ACTOR AND DIRECTOR
MARIO VAN PEEBLES
WITH HIS FATHER, MELVIN, WHO DIRECTED THE 1971
FILM *SWEET SWEETBACK'S BAADASSSSS SONG.*

Yet in another sense the character of Sweetback was no stranger to movies. Throughout the history of American film, white men were aggressors on the screen. *The Birth of a Nation* showed whites brutalizing blacks. Tarzan fought African "natives." Actors like Ronald Reagan, John Wayne, Glenn Ford, and Gary Cooper all bravely battled "savage" Indians, "treacherous" Japanese, and anyone else audacious enough to cross their paths. Gun-packing gangsters like James Cagney, Humphrey Bogart, or Edgar G. Robinson shot their way out of most situations.

Sweetback had numerous counterparts. Melvin Van Peebles had simply decided that it was time for a black character to get in on the action. Van Peebles, who worked in the advertising industry, shot his film on a shoestring budget. (Among his investors was a hot young comedian and television star, Bill Cosby.) Like Oscar Micheaux before him, Van Peebles would resort to "guerrilla filmmaking" to get his movie made.

The film sparked a fiery debate. Many said that it was racist, violent, and crude. Others said it was righteous, revolutionary, and long overdue. Originally, only two theaters in the country, one in Los Angeles, the other in Detroit, agreed to show it. But the film's success was overwhelming.

With *Sweetback*, Van Pebbles revived a tradition that Oscar Micheaux began. He directly addressed his audience. In his opening scene the credits read: "Dedicated to the black community."[1]

Twenty years later Spike Lee, Julie Dash, and Van Peebles's son Mario, would employ this technique at the start of their films. The simple gesture by the senior Van Peebles was a revolutionary move, especially considering the film that followed this opening. Warrington Hudlin, who later produced *House Party*, *Boomerang*, and the television show *Cosmic Slop*, was a teenager in East St. Louis when *Sweetback* was released. He recalled sitting in a darkened theater and reading the opening lines. "I was stunned. What do you mean, 'Dedicated to the black community?' It was very clear that a black man was making this film."[2]

When the film received an X-rating from the motion-picture review board, Van Peebles argued that whites in the film industry were trying to silence a black voice. "The message of *Sweetback*," Van Peebles told one magazine, "is that if you can get it together and stand up to the man, then you can win."[3]

The story exploited many myths about black people. Sweetback establishes his masculinity through superhuman sexuality and violence. Nevertheless, Van Peebles insisted that Sweetback was a renegade. The fact that he stands up to Los Angeles police officers who were mistreating blacks was a revolutionary act. (The 1991 videotaped beating of Rodney King and the 1995 confession of Detective Mark Furhman document this ongoing issue.)

Sweetback was released in 1971. Until the late 1960s it was unthinkable that such a film could be written, much less made. Sweetback disturbed many whites and blacks. At the same time, it showed Hollywood that there was an audience for films that projected different images of African Americans.

SHAFT

*S*weetback was followed by *Shaft*, *Superfly*, and then an avalanche of hastily made, cheap, black action films. Directed by Gordon Parks, Sr., *Shaft* is the story of a black Harlem detective. Played by Richard Roundtree, a popular model with the Ebony Fashion Fair, Shaft is a cool dude. Through his use of camera angles to background detailing, Parks presents Shaft as powerful and appealing. He sports long black leather jackets and walks with a swagger. His pad is swank. Ladies love him. "The man" respects him.

John Shaft became a ghetto folk hero. Parks said he was overjoyed to give black youth a chance to see a cool black guy, similar to James Cagney or Humphrey Bogart. Yet Shaft has the street smarts of a stone-cold ghetto guy like Sweetback. "Hell, yes, there's a place for John Shaft," Parks said. "Ghetto kids were coming downtown to see their hero, Shaft, and here was a black man on the screen that they didn't have to be ashamed of."[4]

But there was a spin to Shaft's mystique. By making Shaft a detective—a cool black detective—Parks presented the antithesis of the glorified white gangster. John Shaft turned the tables on racist assumptions about black men.

The Academy Award-winning soundtrack, composed by Isaac Hayes, underscores just how bad John Shaft is. With a full orchestra accompanying him, Hayes sings: "Who's the man who won't cop out, when there's danger all about?" "Shaft!" a trio of female voices known as Hot Buttered Soul responds.[5]

Shaft was successful, but represented only one side of its director. Gordon Parks, Sr., had built a career as an internationally renowned photographer for *Life* magazine. He was a poet, novelist, and composer. He made his directing debut in 1969 with the autobiographical film *The Learning Tree* and became the first African American director of a feature film to register with the Directors Guild of America. (Maya Angelou became the first African American female screenwriter of a feature film with *Georgia, Georgia* in 1972. She later wrote and directed the film *All Day Long*.)

Set in the Kansas of Parks's youth, *The Learning Tree* is a coming-of-age story about Newt Winger, a boy grappling with death, puppy love, racism, and his own virginity. Some critics said that the story was "too soft." In an era of militancy, the relevancy of Parks's small-town tale was questioned. One producer offered Parks an extraordinary amount of money to change all the black characters to whites. Parks refused. "*The Learning Tree* was the truth of my own childhood," he said. "I would not have compromised that truth for the temper of the times." [6]

Parks hoped that after *The Learning Tree* other blacks would have easier access to the power behind the camera. "[The film] was a resolution of whatever it was that took me from the Kansas cornfield to that big camera crane in Hollywood—the crane that, for so long, had been reserved for whites. Now I hope that other black men would take its long ride into the air." [7]

His son Gordon Parks, Jr., took that long ride into the air. The story that he directed, however, the controversial *Superfly*, was not one that reflected his life. Set in Harlem, *Superfly* is the tale of Priest, a drug dealer who wants to get out of the business, but is prevented by organized crime. Like Shaft, Priest is a street hero, though on the other side of the law. He drives gaudy, customized Cadillacs and wears flowing coats with fur collars. His favorite piece of jewelry is a small spoon used for snorting cocaine. Once again, a musical

THE LEARNING TREE,
DIRECTED BY GORDON
PARKS AND RELEASED IN 1969, WAS BASED ON PARKS'S
AUTOBIOGRAPHICAL NOVEL ABOUT A BOY'S COMING OF AGE.

soundtrack composed by a popular black artist solidified the picture's attraction. Curtis Mayfield's compositions such as "Freddie's Dead" and "Little Child Running Wild" helped Parks depict life in the Harlem drug world.

The film made an impact, especially on young audiences. "Me and my partners decided to become Superfly after we saw the movie," says Narcelle Reedus, a filmmaker based in Atlanta. "We went out and bought the fake-fur hats. I even got a little spoon and put it on a necklace. I pretended that it was a coke spoon."[8] The personas of many of today's gangsta rappers come straight out of *Superfly*: Sir Mix-A-Lot, Too Short, and Ice-T all pay homage to "the ghetto prince."

Superfly outraged black nationalists and traditional civil-rights groups. The National Association for the Advancement of Colored People picketed the film from coast to coast. "We have a huge problem with image," the president of the Detroit branch of the NAACP said. (Detroit was one of the first cities to show *Sweetback*.) "Those movies are in effect telling kids that to make it you've got to kill and use dope. They're not showing that education, compassion, and brotherhood combined with old-fashioned hard work is what it really takes."[9]

THE BLAXPLOITATION ERA

a group of films modeled after *Shaft* and *Superfly* became known as blaxploitation pictures. From 1970 to 1973 nearly fifty such films were churned out. They are usually about sexy, violent, and rebellious macho black men. Athletes-turned-actors Bernie Casey, Jim Brown, and Fred Williamson were popular stars in these cheap dramas that featured blood, guts, and sex. The heroes and heroines of these films are a far cry from Mammy, Uncle Tom, or even Homer Smith. They buck, blast, and fight their way to victory. A racist white gangster meets his death. A corrupt police chief is busted. Unlike the slick gangster films of James Cagney, these movies are very messy. Sexual conquests are frequent.

Pam Grier and Tamara Dobson were the queens of blaxploitation flicks. Grier starred in adventures like *Coffy* and *Sheba Baby.* Dobson was best remembered for her role as the sassy, gun-toting private eye Cleopatra Jones. In the 1990s the Cleopatra Jones look—platform shoes, bell-bottom pants, gargantuan afro, and fake-fur coat—would enjoy a resurgence in popularity.

Black audiences jammed theaters that showed blaxploitation films. "You ain't heard nothing yet until you hear a theater filled with a Saturday night audience of blacks talking back to the screen, telling Jim Brown and Fred Williamson what to do with the Mafia heavies," Sidney Poitier wrote. "I know because…I, too, enjoyed seeing the black guys beating up on the white guys for a change. It was delicious." [10]

The films were profitable, but blacks in Hollywood reaped little of the monetary benefits. Nor did blacks have true creative power. The majority of the producers and directors of these films were white. The studios made films like *Black Caesar, Hell Up in Harlem,* and *The Mack* quickly and on shoe-string budgets. They raked in millions at the box office. During a promotional tour for *The Legend of Nigger Charlie,* D'Urville Martin, who co-starred with Fred Williamson in the western, addressed a group of high school students who asked him about the negative images his films presented. Martin said, "The directors write that s—t as they go along. *The Mack* was so bad that when Richard Pryor watched it with Max Julien (the star) for the first time, they were embarrassed. It was so bad that they cried." [11]

These films thrived on stereotypes. Men were usually depicted as studs. Women were often shown as easy sexual objects. Families were nonexistent. Everyone seemed to live in "the projects," and few seemed to hold legal employment.

Many blacks in the motion-picture industry wondered what would happen when the blaxploitation era came to an end. Gordon Parks, Sr., complained that in the studios' stampede to make these films "with a rash of bad screenplays," [12] they killed what could have been an exciting genre. "I like *The Learning Tree* better than both *Shafts* put together," he said of his films in

1972. "It's a movie about people, complicated people, and of course it had a lot of me in it. After this second *Shaft* film, I'm pulling out of black films as such."[13]

MOVIES ABOUT PEOPLE

blaxploitation pictures were not the only black-oriented films that were produced in the 1970s. A cadre of black filmmakers had quietly been training at film schools across the country. Educational scholarships were one of the fruits of the civil rights movement and the inner-city rebellions of the 1960s. Many of these filmmakers studied at the prestigious film schools of New York University, the University of Southern California, and the University of California at Los Angeles.

Director Michael Schultz was among the best. Several of the feature films he directed during this period are now considered black classics. Among his most popular films were *Cooley High*, *Which Way Is Up?*, *Greased Lightning*, and *Car Wash*.

The autobiographical *Cooley High* was the most touching of Schultz's films. It is the tale of a group of high school chums growing up in the South Side of Chicago. The dialogue and antics in the film are richly black. The characters play "the dozens" (the verbal game of insulting someone's mother) with the skill that characterizes street-corner dialogues. Schultz told the *Washington Post* that most Hollywood executives were caught off guard by the film's success. "It was a complete surprise to the studio. They had no idea how to sell it. It dealt with real kids, it had almost no sex, little violence. They said, 'How do we sell this?' I said, 'How about selling it like a real movie?'"[14]

Which Way Is Up?, *Greased Lightning*, and *Car Wash* featured comedian Richard Pryor. Schultz based *Which Way Is Up?* on the Italian art film *The Seduction of Mimi*. Pryor played all three leading roles. Pryor took a dramatic turn in *Greased Lightning*. This film tells the story of America's first professional race car driver, Wendell Scott. Pryor personally wanted to make the movie. To him, Scott's life represented a story of courage. Scott was a hard-working African American hero, not a ghetto prince like Superfly. (In fact, filming began with Melvin Van Peebles of *Sweetback* fame in the director's chair. He and Pryor fell out over creative differences, and Schultz finished the picture.) Many felt Pryor portrayed Scott with a "black" humanity that was unprecedented on the screen.

RICHARD PRYOR: A HOLLYWOOD ORIGINAL

indeed, to many, Pryor was an original. He began his career as a stand-up comedian on the notorious "chittlin' circuit" for black performers. Eventually, he became a regular act in Las Vegas—until he abandoned his ambitions to become the next Bill Cosby.

Several recordings of his stage routines brought him to national attention. With brazen titles like *That Nigger's Crazy* and *Bicentennial Nigger*, Pryor's albums sold well with blacks and whites. These titles and the often profane language that Pryor used offended some. Others, however, pointed out that Pryor brilliantly exploited the power of racist and offensive language by using it to evoke laughter rather than anger.

Pryor was no less successful in the movies. Simply seeing Pryor on the screen was enough to send audiences into stitches. Journalist Les Payne called him "a comic genius without peer in this humorless age."[15] But he was not a self-effacing clown like Stepin Fetchit. In *The Bingo Long Traveling All-Stars and Motor Kings,* Pryor steals the movie from Billy Dee Williams, the heartthrob who stars in the title role, and James Earl Jones. Pryor plays Charlie Snow, an African American baseball player who desperately wants to make it to the major (white) leagues. During the 1930s, when the film takes place, the major leagues barred blacks from their teams. Charlie assumes a variety of ethnic identities, including that of a Cuban ballplayer, in the hope that a big-time scout will discover him.

COMEDIAN AND ACTOR RICHARD PRYOR,
SHOWN HERE IN *WHICH WAY IS UP?* DIRECTED BY MICHAEL SCHULTZ.

Away from movie sets, Pryor's personal life was a drama of its own. He threw wild parties. He was consumed by drugs. He wrecked automobiles. He fought with girlfriends and ex-wives. Seemingly, Pryor was hell-bent on following in the self-destructive footsteps of Lincoln Perry. Pryor joked that he had nine lives, just like a cat.

In the early 1980s, Pryor went too far. He nearly killed himself free-basing (smoking crystallized cocaine mixed with ether). When he lit a match, the poison exploded. More than fifty percent of his body was burned. In the aftermath, Pryor seemingly laughed in death's face. "When they bury me, they better dig this hole deep, because I may get out of that, too." [16] One year after the fire, Pryor used the tragedy as a hilarious routine in his concert film *Richard Pryor Live on Sunset Strip*.

The notoriety increased Pryor's popularity. He relished superstardom. Still, some felt he wore a mask that grinned and lied. Many blacks thought that Pryor should concern himself with more important racial issues. In response to pressure from the NAACP, Pryor founded a production company, Indigo Films. Although he received $40 million to develop six films, the company went nowhere. Pryor hired his good friend Jim Brown, one of the kings of the blaxploitation era, to run the company. But Pryor did not care about the day-to-day operations of Indigo, which made only one movie, *Jo Jo Dancer, Your Life Is Calling*, a story that had striking resemblances to Pryor's life.

Spike Lee said he understands the pressures that Pryor must have been under. "When we talk about black film, you're carrying the whole burden of the black race on your shoulders...when Richard Pryor got his deal with Indigo, he became the messiah with black people. Jesus Christ...like he was going to be the salvation for all of us. And it's never going to be like that." [17]

To many, Pryor could have been the new Oscar Micheaux, Paul Robeson, and Sidney Poitier all rolled into one. Perhaps Pryor did not want the part. Poitier directed Pryor in the prison comedy *Stir Crazy*. Teamed with white comedian Gene Wilder, the film was a tremendous success. But Pryor battled Poitier on the set. He accused Poitier of mistreating black prisoners who played as extras. Pryor's shenanigans grew outrageous. One day, crew members were joking and started a food fight. A piece of watermelon flew past Pryor's head. He stormed off the set and returned with a pistol. "Throw some watermelon at me now," he dared anyone on the set. [18]

"That Pryor apparently lost his mind in Hollywood, like so many before him, is sad not simply in the way all human loss is sad; it was a tragedy of enormous proportions for African Americans," journalist Nelson George wrote. "His characters were very detailed and always based on reality, yet surreal in a way you might find books by Ralph Ellison, Zora Neale Hurston, or Chester Himes." [19] Eventually, Pryor contracted the degenerative nervous system disorder, multiple sclerosis. His struggle with the disease replaced his career.

FIGHTING FOR THE POWER

During Pryor's rise to stardom, blacks fought to make films from the works of black writers whose genius resembled Pryor's. Ossie Davis directed *Cotton Comes to Harlem*, a tale of comedy and murder based on a story by Chester Himes, the great black mystery writer. This film was of particular significance. For more than thirty years Himes had lived in France as an ex-patriot. He was a key figure in the colony of African American writers that included Frank Yerby, Richard Wright, and James Baldwin. His tale of detective Coffin Ed and his partner, Gravedigger Jones, provided a view of life that a white writer could never hope to capture. It was black camp. "Too many of the works of our best short fiction writers lie unread and even unknown in the forgotten pages of dusty periodicals, newspapers, and magazines," wrote Calvin Herton in his introduction to a collection of Himes's short stories. [20] Black filmmakers would revive Himes on the big screen. Twenty years after Ossie Davis's film, Bill Duke directed *A Rage in Harlem*, another Himes story.

Blacks pressed for power in Hollywood. Sidney Poitier capitalized on his status as a living legend. Along with Barbra Streisand and Robert Redford he became a partner in First Artists Corporation. The three artists entered into contracts with major studios to back the films of their choice. Under this agreement Poitier, Streisand, and Redford produced, wrote, and directed their own projects.

One of Poitier's first films with First Artists Corporation was a western in which he and his friend Harry Belafonte starred, *Buck and the Preacher.* The film was both entertainment and education. It quickly established itself as something more than a run-of-the-mill western. The story takes place in the years following the Civil War. In the late nineteenth century many freedmen headed west to make lives as homesteaders. In what was known as the Great Plains Settlement, blacks settled in Missouri, Nebraska, New Mexico, Texas, Oklahoma, Kansas, Colorado, South Dakota, and North Dakota. Despite their emancipation, however, they were often pursued by bounty hunters who kidnapped them back into sharecropping and, in some instances, even slavery, although it had been abolished. In the opening credits the film's dedication reads: "For the men, women and children who lie in graves as unmarked as their place in history."[21] *Buck and the Preacher* tells the story of these pioneers.

Buck, played by Sidney Poitier, is a guide who leads black settlers to plots of land that they have purchased from the federal government. Blacks trust Buck because he safely delivers them to their land. He has a sixth sense for an ambush in the making. One day he meets a bootlegging preacher, played by Belafonte, of "the high and low order of the holiness persuasion."[22] (Many critics said that this role allowed Belafonte to move beyond the "island boy" image that he had built starring opposite black beauties like Dorothy Dandridge and white actresses like Joan Fontaine and Joan Crawford.) Buck, a serious man, and the preacher, a two-bit hustler, are about as friendly as a rattlesnake and coyote. The preacher cuts a deal with a bounty hunter to doublecross Buck. But eventually his conscience gets the better of him, he confesses, and the plot is foiled.

The film's characters are not the passive, slow-moving blacks of *Gone With the Wind*. These blacks did not tearfully glance over their shoulders as they left the war-ravaged and defeated South behind. They had options, and they knew it. They would risk even death to create a new life for themselves. The threat of violence and lynching was ever present. But nothing could be worse than the life of enslavement they had left behind. At one point Ruby Dee, who plays Buck's wife, screams: "If Canada would have us, I'd go, Buck. I'll walk to the end of the ocean to be free!" [23]

Buck and the Preacher was also unusual for the way it depicted Native Americans. Other Hollywood westerns often showed fearless settlers fighting savage Indians. *Buck and the Preacher* showed an often neglected piece of American history: the relationships between black frontiersmen and Native Americans. Blacks and Indians frequently intermarried. Both groups were distrustful of the "white man." "We wanted black people to see the film and be proud of themselves, be proud of their history," Poitier stressed. "However dishonest, unpleasant, and inhuman had been the depiction of that history by those white men who had written most of the history books that tell us about ourselves, we want the film to say: 'Hey look, there were those of us, and not just a few, who were people of great courage, of great stamina, or great personality, of great convention.'" [24]

Poitier also directed *A Warm December*, a love story about a widowed African American physician who falls in love with an African princess suffering from sickle-cell anemia. Poitier's other films included the comedies *Uptown Saturday Night* and *Let's Do It Again*. The casts of these films read like a who's who of black Hollywood. Poitier was joined by Belafonte, Denise Nicholas, Bill Cosby, Ossie Davis, and other stars.

The cultural awareness prompted by the Black Arts Movement undoubtedly influenced this new wave of black films. Writers and intellectuals such as Ishmael Reed, Lonnie Elder III, Richard Wesley, Charles Fuller, and William Greaves produced work that was strictly based on the black experience. Among the more politically charged films was Ivan Dixon's *The Spook Who Sat by the*

Door. It is the story, penned by writer Sam Greenlee, of a black agent with the Central Intelligence Agency (CIA) who becomes a revolutionary.

Several well-made black films that did not employ black directors were produced during this period. Among the cream of the crop were *Lady Sings the Blues*, a glamorized biography of jazz singer Billie Holiday; *Sounder*, the tale of a sharecropping family whose father is sentenced to work on the chain gang; *Sparkle*, the story of a female singing group; and *Claudine*, a gritty drama about a Harlem welfare mother. In his autobiography, *To Be Loved*, Berry Gordy, the founder of Motown Records, detailed his struggles to make *Lady Sings the Blues* and *Mahogany*, with leading lady Diana Ross. Although Gordy had built one of the most successful record companies in the world, Hollywood studios were reluctant to finance his movies.

A FLOP AND THE FUTURE

the scope of black images on the screen was expanding. Finally it appeared that Hollywood understood what blacks had been saying since the days of race movies. There were plenty of movies to be made about the African American experience.

But one huge flop nearly ruined everything. From Hollywood's point of view, the 1970s ended on a dismal note for black films. The disappointment centered on one film: *The Wiz*, starring Diana Ross, Michael Jackson, and Richard Pryor. The movie cost $24 million to make in 1978. It was directed by white filmmaker Sidney Lumet (the son-in-law of Lena Horne). It was the most expensive black movie at that time. (In 1992, Spike Lee's *Malcolm X* would double this price tag.)

The Wiz was based on *The Wizard of Oz*, the 1939 film classic starring Judy Garland. She played Dorothy, a white farm girl from Kansas, who is blown into the land of Oz by a twister. In 1975, *The Wiz* had been presented on Broadway in an all-black version that mirrored the original story line. Young Stephanie Mills, a powerhouse of a soul singer, starred. The stage version,

BASED ON THE 1939 FILM CLASSIC
THE WIZARD OF OZ, THE 1978 FILM
THE WIZ, DIRECTED BY SIDNEY LUMET, STARRED (FROM LEFT TO RIGHT)
TED ROSS, MICHAEL JACKSON, DIANA ROSS, AND NIPSEY RUSSELL.

which featured new music and a much funkier spin than the original movie, had been a huge success. The storyline of the film *The Wiz* was changed to accommodate Ross. Dorothy became a shy twenty-four-year-old Harlem schoolteacher. Many did not find Ross believable in the role, however. Over the years, Ross had presented herself as a glamorous Hollywood star. In her publicity stills she was photographed in the same manner as the white actress Jean Harlow and Josephine Baker, the enchanting Negress who took Paris by storm in the 1920s. Ross was all furs, feathers, and flowing hair. Few could picture her as a shy schoolteacher.

The rest of the all-star cast, however, excelled. Lena Horne, as Glinda the Good Witch of the West, stole the show with a stirring rendition of "Believe in Yourself." Michael Jackson, on the eve of his superstardom, played the Scarecrow, filling the screen with funky dance steps. Richard Pryor played a jittery Wizard of Oz. He was a jiving, no-good guy who hoodwinked the munchkins, the trusting people of Emerald City.

The Wiz required that white America be open to a new interpretation of a story that was as American as mom's apple pie. The stretch was too great for many people to make, and the movie flopped. In the wake of this fiasco many people predicted that Hollywood would be reluctant to finance another black film of this magnitude.

But there were other cinematic visions on the horizon. Sidney Poitier was optimistic. "We're going to have to make most of our own films." he said. "I think we should no longer expect the white filmmaker to be the champion of our dreams." Poitier saw self-created opportunities that would allow ambitious filmmakers to work outside the Hollywood system. "So black filmmakers,…be ready, stay alert," he championed. "Don't let 'the man' beat you on your own home ground." [25]

A new breed of black filmmakers was waiting in the wings. They had plenty of education, business savvy, and a vision of how blacks should appear on the screen. In short, they were their own men and women. They knew how they wanted the world to see them.

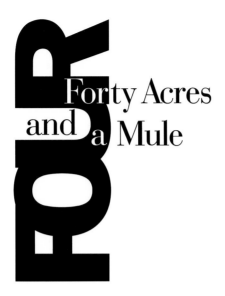

FOUR

Forty Acres and a Mule

For decades, blacks in the film industry have referred to Hollywood as "the plantation." They said that Hollywood's treatment of black people on the screen and within the industry was deplorable. Hollywood was also a slang term used by blacks to indicate "selling out" or denying one's roots. When you "went Hollywood," you changed. You switched political parties. Perhaps you moved into a more upscale, white neighborhood. Maybe you took on a new set of friends and abandoned your old crew. You moved out of "the hood."

Spike Lee was among the first black filmmakers to win respect in Hollywood without "going Hollywood." Lee made it clear that his main business with Hollywood was to make movies. He had little interest in the flamboyant lifestyles that the film industry offered.

To appreciate Lee's achievements, consider the fifteen years between Melvin Van Peebles's *Sweet Sweetback's Baadasssss Song* and Spike Lee's first major feature film, *She's Gotta Have It*. Except for Poitier, Parks, and

Schultz, there were few black directors of feature films. Although black-oriented films made money, blacks had no control over the kinds of movies that were made. Many black actors complained that they were forced to take the stereotypical roles of prostitutes, pimps, drug dealers, maids, and butlers to pay their rent. It was a take-it-or-leave-it situation.

Lee was the champion in a film movement that stressed independent financing and creative control, or "final edits." These new filmmakers used the Hollywood system for distribution purposes only. If they could not get their films distributed by Hollywood, they often went to European film distributors. They did not wait for Hollywood to call them. Unlike Lincoln Perry, they were not interested in "getting permission" to make their films. They asked themselves, "How can we get this done on our own" rather than "How do we deal with white studios for support?" They were film-school graduates. They understood the nuts and bolts of both the creative and the business sides of moviemaking. They were a new breed of blacks with a new perspective.

SHAPED BY THEIR • TIME

In the 1980s, blacks made numerous social, cultural, political, and economic advances. The Reverend Jesse Jackson, an aide to Dr. Martin Luther King, Jr., at the time of his death, was the first black to be a serious contender for the U.S. presidency. He ran for the office in 1984 and 1988. Jackson has a strong presence and is an excellent orator. The preacher was determined. He would not quit. He campaigned on a "Rainbow Coalition" platform, one that included all Americans, regardless of race, religion, disability, or sexual preference.

For blacks, Jackson's candidacy encouraged large-scale voter registration. After the assassinations of Dr. King and Malcolm X in the 1960s, most blacks in the ghetto, as well as middle-class blacks, were cynical. Jackson's campaign slogan was "Keep Hope Alive!" The number of new black voters swelled. Although Jackson did not win the election, there were tremendous payoffs for black America. At the local and state levels the number of black elected officials increased dramatically, a result of the impressive new numbers of registered voters.

Elsewhere in black life other gains were made. Dr. Mae Jemison became the country's first female African American astronaut. Anchorman Bryant Gumble dominated the morning news on *The Today Show*. Charming and impeccably dressed, but disarmingly analytical, Gumble presented a new image of the educated black. "He must have something going on if white folk will watch him every morning," one African American senior citizen said. [1]

Each day millions of Americans tuned into *The Oprah Winfrey Show*. Dark-skinned Winfrey became the queen of afternoon talk shows, successful on her own terms. (Winfrey would be nominated for an Academy Award for her role as Sophia in the film *The Color Purple*. She would also produce numerous television films including *The Women of Brewster Place*, based on the best-selling novel by Gloria Naylor.)

Blacks also dominated sports and entertainment. Earvin "Magic" Johnson led the Los Angeles Lakers to five championships in the National Basketball Association. Michael Jordan of the Chicago Bulls was a one-man phenomenon, the most breathtaking basketball player that the world had ever seen.

Out of New Orleans the Marsalis brothers, Wynton and Branford, took their trumpet and saxophone and resurrected "real" jazz. They found the best young musicians to fill out their band. Wynton recorded with operatic diva Kathleen Battle. Branford collaborated with the pop artist, Sting, and later formed Buck Shot Le Fonque, his own hip-hop jazz band.

In literature there was an explosion of new black fiction. Black women like Maya Angelou, Gloria Naylor, Toni Morrison, Paule Marshall, Alice Walker, and playwright and novelist Ntozake Shange led the way.

Perhaps the biggest cultural explosion came from young people in the inner city. They created rap music, and it was a force to be reckoned with.

AMONG THE MANY
PROMINENT BLACK
ARTISTS OF THE 1980S WERE THE MUSICIAN
BROTHERS WYNTON AND BRANFORD MARSALIS.

Rap is urban poetry. With words recited over rhythms, the art form became a worldwide phenomenon. Queen Latifah, Naughty by Nature, Ice Cube, Arrested Development, Yo-Yo, and Snoop Doggy Dogg became superstars and, for better or worse, role models.

But rap is more than just music. It is also hip-hop, the culture that accompanies it. Hip-hop, a contemporary term taken from bebop, the jazz music of the 1950s, was a world unto itself. Hip-hop has a language, a value system, and an image that are original. Some champions of the culture call it "ghettocentric." It is the antithesis of mainstream America, yet it captured broad attention.

Dancehall was the cousin of hip-hop. Straight out of the ghettos of Kingston, Jamaica, this hard-edged music featured the Caribbean equivalent of American rappers. Dancehall "dons" like Shabba Ranks, Super Cat, and Red Fox covered many topics in their music. They featured pan-Africanism (influenced by the teachings of Marcus Garvey, who was Jamaican), politics (local and international), and slackness (double-entendre sexual lyrics). Like rap, Dancehall spread like wildfire. The cultural exchange between these two urban art forms was intense.

This was the world that aspiring young black filmmakers knew. All around them African Americans were making their own way. The filmmakers seemed to embody a popular slogan of Dr. Benjamin Mays, president emeritus of Morehouse College: "I will find a way or make one."[2]

SPIKE LEE'S ROOTS

Lee and other black filmmakers who followed him came to prominence in this atmosphere of self-empowerment. For Spike Lee, a sense of identity is crucial to creativity. Lee's identity is tied to his childhood, education, and roots in Brooklyn, New York.

The oldest of five children, Shelton Jackson Lee was born in Atlanta, Georgia, on March 20, 1957. His father, Bill Lee, was a noted acoustic bassist on

the folk-music scene. His mother, Jacquelyn Shelton Lee, was a schoolteacher. The Lees lived briefly in Chicago and finally settled in Brooklyn. Jacquelyn Lee died of cancer in 1976. (Lee would tell the story of the last summer of his mother's life in the film *Crooklyn*.) Lee's mother nicknamed him Spike when he was a baby. According to Lee, he was a rough-and-tumble sort of child, forever skinning a knee or busting his lip.

He was also an organizer. It didn't matter if it was a baseball game or a picnic, Lee was usually at the helm. His knack for bringing people together to achieve a common goal would prove invaluable when he decided to become a filmmaker. "I always organized the teams on our block. I was always the one to take the lead. When I went to Morehouse, there hadn't been an intramural softball team in ten years. I organized that. When you're a filmmaker what you're really doing is motivating people. That's a gift I have."[3]

Lee learned to separate himself from what he considered lowbrow pop black culture. As a youngster Lee never had much use for blaxploitation films. He credited his father with distancing him from films like *J. D.'s Revenge*. Instead, Lee was into "art films" and jazz. "I'm not saying I was a fully developed film connoisseur back then, but because of my father I had been weaned not just on art, but the purer forms of art. I didn't see those kind[s] of films until much later."[4] Lee loved the films of Akira Kurosawa, the internationally renowned Japanese filmmaker. Kurosawa's classic films, such as *Rashomon* and *The Seventh Samurai*, held much more fascination for Lee than any cheaply made ghetto flick.

"It really is not surprising that Spike Lee, and later John Singleton, would not be influenced by the blaxploitation film," said Clayton Riley. "They were serious young film scholars. Blaxploitation films were not scholarly films. But you can't deny the significance of these films. Most gangster rappers would be influenced by blaxploitation movies. Why, Big Daddy Kane, the rapper, boasts the world's largest collection of blaxploitation pictures."[5]

Lee was a strong-willed individual. He never followed the crowd. He inherited his assertiveness from his ancestors. With a half smile on his face, Lee proudly told the story. "My great great great great grandfather Mike and his wife Phoebe were slaves. They were broken up. Mike worked three or four years to buy his freedom and walked from South Carolina to Alabama to reunite with his wife and family. I'm a descendant of him. That's my family. We've always been very strong, very proud, fearless, and intelligent."[6] In the 1930s, Zimmie Shelton, Lee's grandmother, sold black dolls and greeting cards that she designed herself. "It astounds me that she had the foresight to see [the need for] that stuff even back then."[7]

Given his family's history, it comes as no surprise that Lee often rattled the nerves of the Hollywood establishment. Whites in positions of authority tend to consider blacks like Lee "difficult." Hollywood is no exception. In Hollywood, conformity is the route to success. Spike Lee does not have the credentials of a conformist. He is nobody's yes man. When he made his mark in the film world, many critics attempted to characterize him as an "angry black man." Some called him a small man with a big ego. Lee responded that his white critics were racist. His black critics, he said, were "handkerchief head wearing Negroes," a term that Malcolm X often used. "I am simply an educated black man," Lee said. "That scares the s—t out of a whole lot of people."[8]

In 1975, Lee entered Morehouse College, the most prestigious college in the world for black men. He had quite a tradition to uphold. Lee's great grand-father founded Snow Hill Institute in Alabama. His mother attended Spelman, the sister college to Morehouse. Years later Lee's office in Fort Greene, Brooklyn, became a shrine to the African American intellectual tradition. He collected rare papers of historical figures like Booker T. Washington, Marcus Garvey, Langston Hughes, and Ralph Ellison. He also framed the film posters of Oscar Micheaux.

Lee had a good time at Morehouse. He hosted a jazz show on the campus radio station and organized the Morehouse homecoming. He decided that film would be his area of concentration.

During the summer of 1979, Lee interned at Columbia Pictures in Los Angeles. That fall he began studies at the prestigious film school at New York University. Lee wanted to attend a film school close to his Brooklyn base. "I had more resources at my disposal," the pragmatic Lee explained. "The money I would spend on room and board, I spent to make films."[9]

During his first year at NYU, Lee nearly created a civil war in the film department with his ten-minute film *The Answer.* It is the story of a young black writer who is assigned to update *The Birth of a Nation.* The short film was not kind to Griffith, who was now enshrined in Hollywood and film schools as "the father of American cinema." The faculty was not pleased with Lee's challenge of the "facts," but Lee refused to back down. He was threatened with expulsion. The faculty was divided on the artistic merit and technical competence of Lee's work. Still, if he were kicked out of the program, Lee promised to take legal action. He'd charge NYU with bias. Even as a film student Lee served notice that nobody could walk over him.

His next two years were very busy. He won a scholarship and became a teaching assistant. He also worked in a film lab. His senior project in 1982 was called *Joe's Bed-Stuy Barbershop: We Cut Heads.* The film is a humorous look at a Brooklyn barbershop that fronts for a numbers operation. The hour-long film won Lee a student Academy Award. One reviewer noted that in contrast to the blaxploitation films ten years earlier, Joe's offered "a friendly portrait of black folkways." [10]

WE ARE FAMILY

to appreciate Lee's rise from his student days to international acclaim, it is important to remember that Lee had a strong support system within his family and the black Brooklyn community. "Film is a joint effort," stressed Morgan Freeman, the veteran actor and director of *Bopha!*, a South African drama that Arsenio Hall produced. "You simply don't make movies by yourself. You need all kinds of help." [11]

Lee's achievements represent the results of many joint efforts. Like his childhood activities, Lee carefully organized his career. After completing his film studies at NYU, Lee set up his production company, calling it Forty Acres and a Mule Filmworks. The name comes from a clause in the Freedmen's Bureau Act of 1865, which promised all newly emancipated Negro adult males, or freedmen, land and a beast with which to till the soil and build an American dream for their families. Lee enlisted several family members and longtime associates in his new venture. College buddy Monty Ross, the co-producer of every Spike Lee "joint," as he calls his pictures, was integral from the beginning. Cinematographer Ernest Dickerson has given the films their huge, lush visuals. David Lee, Spike's brother, has been the still photographer on all of the movies. His dad wrote the music for many of the films. His sister Joie has had supporting roles in several films and was co-author of the script for *Crooklyn.*

Ross recalled sitting with Lee on the porch of Lee's grandmother's house during their student days at Morehouse College. The two young men day-dreamed of making great movies. They knew that they'd have to work outside of the mainstream and that they would need their own money. "All media, including film, as popular as it is, has been one of the slowest outlets in allowing blacks to control the reflected image of their culture, to control the expressions of themselves. They always want to censor it to their liking, or water it down," Ross wrote in *By Any Means Necessary: The Trials and Tribulations of Making Malcolm X.*[12]

Zimmie Shelton was one of the earliest supporters of Lee's dream. Over the years she would invest nearly $20,000 into her grandson's various projects. "My grandmother paid my way through film school," Lee recalled. Mrs. Shelton provided her grandson with a patient, listening ear. "She always had complete faith in me."[13] Writer Nelson George also offered Lee moral encouragement and financial assistance. George took part of his earnings from a "quickie" biography he had written of Michael Jackson and invested it in *She's Gotta Have It.* Lee had presented shorts of the film to many black businessmen. Most couldn't understand why the movie was shot in black and white. "What bothered me the most was the lack of imagination by these black folks with cash," George wrote. "The film, they felt, couldn't work because Hollywood hadn't done it."[14]

Lee's cinematic vision of life in the African American community was unique from the beginning. His is an intimate perspective rooted in the same Brooklyn neighborhood where he grew up, far from Hollywood in many ways. Fort Greene is a tree-lined community of brownstones, home to hardworking African Americans, Jamaicans, Haitians, Nigerians, Senegalese, Dominicans, and Puerto Ricans. The dynamics of this rainbow community and others in Brooklyn imbue Lee's films.

1ee's first feature film was shot in a record fourteen days on a budget of $175,000, dirt cheap by Hollywood standards. He poured every penny he had into the film. At one point the lab processing the film threatened to sell the master copy of *She's Gotta Have It* if Lee didn't come up with the $2,000 he owed them. Surely, Oscar Micheaux had days like this. Luckily, a friend paid the bill. Lee called this high-stress, low-cash approach to movie making "guerrilla filmmaking."

In the summer of 1986 the Black Filmmakers Foundation (BFF) hosted the East Coast premier of *She's Gotta Have It.* (BFF, a nonprofit organization supporting independent black filmmakers, was founded in 1978 by Warrington and Reggie Hudlin, who directed *House Party* and *Boomerang*.) On opening night, the lines were long, and advance tickets were a must. Shot in black and white, *She's Gotta Have It* became the hip New York event of the season. Anyone who was on the cutting edge of cool had to check out *She's Gotta Have It* at the artsy Lincoln Center Plaza Cinema. Afterward moviegoers went to coffeehouses and talked about the film over cappuccino and French pastry. They studied the camera angles, analyzed the characters, replayed the dialogue, and discussed the film's relevancy to the African American experience. This certainly was not the kind of response that audiences had to blaxploitation films. Most African Americans didn't know anyone like Pam Grier's Coffy. But most people knew the characters in *She's Gotta Have It.*

The movie tells the story of Nola Darling, an attractive graphic artist, who has three lovers: the earnest Jamie Overstreet, the conceited Greer Childs, and the homeboy bicycle messenger, Mars Blackmon, who wears Air Jordans, athletic jerseys, and a gaudy nameplate necklace.

The film is dedicated to the memory of Zora Neale Hurston, the most prominent female writer of the Harlem Renaissance during the 1920s and the 1930s. Hurston was a peer of Langston Hughes, Claude McKay, and Countee

Cullen. She was a rebel, a feminist in the days when feminism, particularly in the black community, was not fashionable.

The film opens with the narrator's reading of a passage from Hurston's most popular book, *Their Eyes Were Watching God:* "Ships at a distance have every man's wish on board. For some they come in with the tide. For others they sail forever on the horizon, never out of sight, never landing until the watcher runs his eyes away in resignation, his dreams mocked to death by time. This is the life of men. Now, women forget all those things they don't want to remember, and remember everything they don't want to forget. The dream is the truth. Then they act and do things accordingly."[18]

The theme of a woman's having to choose between love-struck men is nothing new. But no one had ever told the tale in quite this way. *She's Gotta Have It* is a genuinely African American story. Some scenes have the look of a documentary. The characters speak directly to the camera and report their feelings. Jamie is dependable and responsive to Nola, but he places limits on her. Greer is a smug, social-climbing "buppie" (black urban professional) who wants Nola to buy into his self-absorbed lifestyle. Blackmon, played by Lee, offers comic relief to Nola and the viewer. None of these men values the others, nor can see what Nola sees in them.

Nola represents a new breed of black woman. Finding a husband is clearly not her priority. She visits a therapist, also black and female, who assures her that her diverse sexual interests are normal. The relationship between Nola and her therapist is itself taboo. Many blacks have shunned therapy, thinking "only white folks need that mess." In the end, having made her choice and comfortable with it, Nola concludes, "It's about control. My body, my mind. Who's gonna own it? Them or me?"[19]

She's Gotta Have It was a smash. The film won the coveted *Prix de Jeunesse* award at the prestigious international Cannes Film Festival. With the film's success, major studios opened their doors to Lee, who insisted on maintaining creative control of his work. No studio honcho or technical assistant could look over his shoulder and "make suggestions." Lee had captured Hollywood's attention and was going to proceed on his own terms.

SCHOOL DAZE

With his second film, *School Daze*, Lee again courted controversy, particularly within the black community. The film takes place at Mission College, an all-black campus that closely resembles Spike Lee's alma mater, Morehouse College. The central themes are color, class, conformity, and solidarity. *School Daze* is the story of a homecoming weekend at Mission College. The pledgees of two rival fraternities are about to "cross the burning sands" into membership. To join the brotherhood, pledges must be willing to do anything and everything that the "big brothers" request.

Lee plays Halfpint, a pledge who is willing to go to any lengths to belong to "the brotherhood." Throughout the film the characters pair off along color lines. The dark-skinned female students, the "Jigaboos," clash with the light-skinned sorority, the "Wannabees." "Da Fellas," a group of strong-willed, politically active young men, tangle with the bourgeois brothers of Gamma Phi Gamma.

Lee set out to show the absurdity and viciousness of color and class prejudice in black America. One scene features the Wannabee sisters and the Jigaboos as mammies in an elaborate musical-production number, taunting one another about their hair. The Wannabees with flowing locks (is it real, is it weaved, or is it pressed at night?) mask their faces with funeral-home hand fans bearing the smiling, kerchief-topped head of Hattie McDaniel.

This scene represented Lee's two-fisted jab at Hollywood and black America. Lee's swipe at Hollywood was for its spectacular waste of McDaniel's talents and for projecting Mammy as the essence of black womanhood. Lee's critique of the African American community was based on its attitudes about physical appearance. The image of Hattie McDaniel was the very last that a Wannabee sister would ever assume. To be hefty and dark-skinned would be the ultimate nightmare for these light-skinned women.

In another scene, a group of working-class black men ("local yokels") confront Da Fellas in a Kentucky Fried Chicken restaurant. The college boys need a salt shaker. When one of them asks to use the shaker on the table packed with boys from the hood, the insults fly. The locals accuse the students of taking their jobs. One of the locals, played by Samuel L. Jackson, asks whether Dap, one of Da Fellas, is black. "Don't ever question the fact whether I'm black," he answers. "In fact, I was gonna ask your country 'bama [Alabama] ass why you got those drip-drip chemicals in your hair." This brief scene of pure black American "dogging" captures the feelings of contempt between college students and the residents of the ghettos surrounding black universities. The locals claim that "Y'all niggers. And you're gonna be niggers. Forever. Just like us." Dap steps up close, right in the local's face, and says, in measured syllables, "You're not niggers." [20]

Lee concludes his exposé of the self-destructive divisiveness of black America with Dap running all over campus and then toward the camera to look directly into it, while he shouts over and over, "Waaaaaake-uuup!"

After getting wind of the script's content, the Morehouse administration, which had originally welcomed the idea of its famous alumnus filming on campus, asked Lee to leave. Lee refused to let anyone, even the president of Morehouse, read the script. The administration felt that Lee was about to air the race's dirty laundry in public. Lee's response was flippant. "Anyone who went to a black college knows that s——t happens. What's the big deal?" [21]

School Daze was finally filmed nearby at Atlanta University. Among the graduate school's most illustrious faculty was W. E. B. Du Bois, who founded AU's prestigious school of social work. In 1915 it had been Du Bois who led the voices of protest against *The Birth of a Nation.*

DO THE RIGHT THING

In his third film, Lee turned his lens from examining color prejudice within the black community to black-white relations. *Do the Right Thing* is set on a hot summer day in the Bedford-Stuyvesant section of Brooklyn. In part, the inspiration for the film came from an episode of the 1960s television series *The Twilight Zone.* A scientist is doing an experiment on heat-induced violence. He speculates that people are more likely to commit murders when the temperature exceeds 95 degrees. Ultimately, the jittery scientist is proven

SPIKE LEE AND DANNY AIELLO IN *DO THE RIGHT THING*, A FILM ABOUT INTERRACIAL TENSIONS IN A NEIGHBORHOOD IN BROOKLYN.

right when the temperature reaches 96 degrees and he is murdered. The story made a lasting impression on the young Spike Lee.

Do the Right Thing centers on the tension between an Italian family that owns Sal's Famous Pizzeria and their black customers. Buggin' Out, the black neighborhood militant, confronts Sal about the lack of African American role models on the pizzeria's "Wall of Fame." The wall is filled with photos of prominent Italian Americans, including baseball legend Joe DiMaggio, champion boxer Rocky Marciano, actress Sophia Loren, singers Perry Como, Frank Sinatra, and Luciano Pavarotti, and Mario Cuomo, then the governor of New York State. "Put some brothers up on this wall. We want Malcolm X, Angela Davis, Michael Jordan, tomorrow!" Buggin' Out adds that residents will boycott his establishment if the photos on the wall don't change. "This is my pizzeria," Sal informs Buggin' Out.[22]

The tension escalates through the day and climaxes in the murder by the police of Radio Rahim, a young man whose constant companion is a boom box. A riot erupts, and Sal's business is burned to the ground.

Released in 1989, soon after Yusef Hawkins, a black youth, was beaten to death by a mob in the predominantly Italian neighborhood of Bensonhurst, Brooklyn, the film forced viewers to confront the terrible and potentially deadly state of race relations. It exposed the anger, hatred, and suspicion that exist between blacks and whites and that are often sugar-coated by the media and politicians. It also examined the fragile terms on which various ethnic groups coexist. Rosie Perez plays Spike Lee's girlfriend. She is a lone Puerto Rican in an all-black Brooklyn neighborhood. Like Sal and his sons, a family of Korean merchants works in the neighborhood and runs its business in an uneasy existence.

Lee had America where he wanted it—squirming over the implications of his work while debating its artistic and social merit. The movie was hailed as an American masterpiece. It took top honors in many of the world's major film competitions. Lee was nominated in two categories for the Oscars: Best Original Screenplay and Best Director. The Los Angeles Film Critics Association bestowed the Best Director award on Lee, and Ernest Dickerson, his cameraman, was nominated for Best Cinematographer.

Many critics suggested that Lee's film would incite riots. Lee fired back that misguided justice caused uprisings. "Verdicts like in the Rodney King trial cause riots, not movies like *Do the Right Thing*," Lee told one of his longtime critics.[23] This was a new level of self-assuredness for a black filmmaker.

Lee was everywhere. He addressed his critics in written editorials, on talk shows, and in panel discussions on college campuses around the country. Some called him arrogant. Some labeled him a racist. Some dismissed him as a "motor mouth." Others accused him of being a bad brother. But hordes of journalists had never asked Oscar Micheaux what he thought about any social issues. The work of Gordon Parks, Michael Schultz, and Melvin Van Peebles had never sparked such intense debate.

The film's urgency was underscored by a hip-hop soundtrack that featured Public Enemy, then the reigning rap group. The group contributed the film's theme song "Fight the Power":

From the heart
It's a start, a work of art
To revolutionize, we make a change, nothin' strange
People people, we are the same
No we're not the same
'Cause we don't know the game
What we need is awareness, we can't get careless
You say what is this?
My beloved, let's get down to business
Mental self-defensive fitness
Bum rush the show
You gotta go for what you know
To make everybody see, in order to fight
the powers that be [24]

In *Jungle Fever*, Lee explored the Pandora's box of interracial relation-ships. Wesley Snipes plays a successful architect who leaves his mulatto wife for an Italian secretary who works in his office. *Fever*'s strongest dramatic moments, however, deal with its secondary theme—the crack-cocaine epi-demic in black America. Samuel L. Jackson plays a crack head whose addic-tion ultimately destroys his family. In a brutally stunning sequence, Lee creates a pathetic scene inside a cavernous crack house. As addicts smoke their trea-sured poison, "Living for the City," the 1970s classic by Stevie Wonder, blares in the background.

When the Italian family quarrels in *Jungle Fever*, it is authentic because he knows such scenes personally. "Spike got us down pat," Nicholas Torello, a Brooklyn-born Italian graphic artist said. "That's how working-class Italians have family arguments."[15]

Lee's movies are magic because they are not Hollywood formulas. His inspiration comes from a place far from the air-conditioned conference rooms where executives dream up marketable myths, where fiction substitutes for reality, where, as in the film *Hollywood Shuffle*, a movie mogul can demand, "Get me Eddie Murphy, or an Eddie Murphy type."[16]

Neighborhood dramas, touched with comedy and irony, are Lee's forte. Spike Lee's "joints" tell stories about everyday folks, many of them "black to the bone," who ride the bus, buy groceries, or take their kids to the barbershop. Lee's movies are the sort that Sidney Poitier lamented that he did not have the power to make in the 1960s. They are the sort that Richard Pryor possessed the power to make during the height of his popularity. Spike Lee's characters live in black America: Mookie, the trifling pizza delivery man; Mars Blackmon, a diehard New York Knicks fanatic; Rahim, whose boom box can be heard a block away; and Mother Sister, the woman in the housecoat who leans out her window and surveys the comings and goings of everyone on the block. Lee's characters talk and act like real people.

"[They] come about," novelist Charles Johnson commented, "because Mr. Lee listens, and listens extremely well, to what the folk are saying when they don't think anyone is watching them."[17]

Mo' Better Blues is Lee's slick homage to jazz. In his debut performance under Lee's direction, Denzel Washington portrays Bleek, a trumpeter and ladies' man. Eventually tragedy forces Bleek to abandon his promising career. Some critics blasted Lee for presenting jazz musicians in a romanticized environment. A feisty Lee responded that contrary to popular myth, not all jazz is performed in hovels and played by nodding drug addicts.

DENZEL WASHINGTON
STARRED IN LEE'S 1990 TRIBUTE TO JAZZ, *MO' BETTER BLUES*.

Spike Lee had plenty of powers to contend with as he worked to bring the life of Malcolm X to the screen. In many respects the rise of Malcolm X to the forefront of the black consciousness movement of the 1960s was white America's worst nightmare. In the hearts and minds of many whites, Martin Luther King, Jr., a Christian minister, was a moderate. Malcolm, a minister with the separatist Nation of Islam, was considered dangerous.

Dr. Cornel West, professor of philosophy and Afro-American studies at Harvard University, explained:

> Malcolm X articulated black rage in a manner unprecedented in American history. His style of communicating this black rage bespoke a boiling urgency and an audacious sincerity. The substance of what he had said highlighted the chronic refusal of most Americans to acknowledge the sheer absurdity that confronts human beings of African descent in this country—the incessant assault on black intelligence, beauty, character and possibility. His profound commitment to affirm black humanity at any cost and his tremendous courage to accent the hypocrisy of American society made Malcolm X the prophet of black rage—then and now.[25]

Lee was much less intellectual about Malcolm's place in American history. "There are still a lot of black people, older black people, who believe that Malcolm X was crazy. That he was a detriment to his race," Lee told *L.A. Style.*[26]

Earlier attempts to bring Malcolm X's extraordinary story to the screen had stalled. In 1968, at the height of the Black Power Movement, writer James Baldwin took up residence in Hollywood to write the screenplay for what would eventually become *Malcolm X.* A "technical assistant" (who was white) was assigned to work with Baldwin. Every scene that Baldwin wrote, the so-called assistant rewrote. In effect, Baldwin labored under a creative overseer who "translated" his scenes. Baldwin was asked to downplay the significance of Malcolm's visit to Mecca, the holy city of Islam. Most outrageous was the studio's insistence that Malcolm be portrayed as a bitter man because he had been betrayed by so many blacks.

The process was frustrating, another attempt to distort the African American experience. As a writer, Baldwin had worked out of Paris and New York City. Hollywood was an alien experience to him. "I had never before seen this machinery at such close quarter, and I confess that I was both fascinated and challenged," he wrote.[27] Baldwin contested the studio's efforts to corrupt his screenplay. It was obvious that the studio wanted a big-name black writer like Baldwin, who was also a good friend of Malcolm, associated with the project. But Hollywood really was not interested in the screenplay he wrote. (One Hollywood insider charged that Baldwin could not finish the script because he had a serious drinking problem.) Baldwin was only too happy when his "Hollywood sentence" drew to a close. He said he'd rather be horsewhipped than to relive the nightmare of Hollywood.

What Baldwin left behind was a strong screenplay. In the credits for the 1992 Lee production, Baldwin would be listed as the primary writer. Lee came to the project better armed for battle than Baldwin. Where Baldwin had been a lone black man pitted against Hollywood, Lee had more power at his disposal. But his task was not an easy one.

First, he had to wrestle the project from director Norman Jewison. Warner Brothers Pictures had secured Jewison, a white man who had successfully made movies featuring blacks, to direct *Malcolm X*. In 1967, Jewison had directed *In the Heat of the Night*. The film starred Sidney Poitier as a Philadelphia detective who passes through a southern town and finds himself in the middle of a murder investigation. The movie won five Oscars. Jewison's latest film, *A Soldier's Story*, featuring a promising young actor named Denzel Washington, was a tale of black-white tensions on a small army base in the South. It had been critically acclaimed. Jewison clearly had credentials for directing black actors. Lee questioned, however, if Jewison was really the best man for the job.

Lee contended that a white director couldn't do justice to the story. Like millions of people of African descent throughout the world, Lee considered

The Autobiography of Malcolm X (along with *The Souls of Black Folk* by W. E. B. Du Bois and Booker T. Washington's *Up From Slavery*) among the most important books of the twentieth century about the black experience. Written with Alex Haley, the author of *Roots*, Malcolm's autobiography is one of the best-selling books in publishing history. Lee pointed out that Hollywood had a track record of diminishing the power and presence of black characters in favor of white characters in films on black subjects. In *Glory*, the tale of the brave men of the 54th Colored Infantry, the first black division to fight in the Civil War, the story is told through the eyes of white commanders. Even the presence of Frederick Douglass, the great abolitionist, is minor. In *Cry Freedom*, Sir Richard Attenborough directed the story of South African anti-apartheid activist Stephen Biko so that it ends up as the getaway tale of the slain Biko's white friend, journalist Donald Woods. This result was very disappointing to many.

Lee was not going to have a white director at the helm of *Malcolm X*. He maintained that he and he alone had earned the right to direct this film so fundamental to African Americans. Lee had a box-office track record. He was the most successful black director in history. According to Lee:

> Malcolm X is really an example of the African American experience. I felt it needed a confident African American director. Spike Lee is not saying that only Chinese people can direct Chinese films, that only black people can direct black films, or that only white people can direct white films. I don't think it should be that way, but there are specific cases where because of your background, because you know the subject matter, it enhances your work. This film needed someone who doesn't have to read a book to know what it is to be called a nigger in this country.[28]

"If you have a good story, what does it matter what color the director is?" Jewison told *The New York Times*.[29] Lee held his ground. His action represented one of the few instances in which a black filmmaker stood up to Hollywood for artistic control and won. This was high stakes, hardball, big-money

SPIKE LEE'S FILM *MALCOLM X*,
STARRING DENZEL WASHINGTON,
WAS BASED ON THE BLACK LEADER'S AUTOBIOGRAPHY, CO-WRITTEN
WITH ALEX HALEY, THE AUTHOR OF *ROOTS*. LEE CONSIDERS THIS WORK,
WHICH TOOK TWO YEARS TO MAKE, HIS TOUR DE FORCE.

movie politics. In the end Jewison diplomatically stepped aside and wished the best for the production.

PREPRODUCTION AND MORE POLITICS

To prepare for the film, Lee conducted extensive research. He interviewed hundreds of Malcolm's family members, friends, and associates, including his widow, Dr. Betty Shabazz, his daughters, his siblings, and Minister Louis Farrakhan, the head of the Nation of Islam. Lee soon discovered that each source had different memories of Malcolm. Some of Malcolm's siblings recalled his warmth and sense of humor. Other siblings claimed that Malcolm exaggerated his days as a hustler. Betty Shabazz grew annoyed when Lee gently asked her if she and her late husband ever argued. Shabazz insisted that they had not. Lee was bothered. "Now what married couple in the history of the world had never had an argument?" Lee asked.[30] He wanted the film to capture the reality of Malcolm's life, not the myths. However, he was sensitive to Shabazz's pain. After all, she had seen her husband gunned down before her eyes, and she had raised six daughters by herself.

The most daunting task was Lee's visit to the Nation of Islam headquarters in Chicago. He had to talk to Minister Louis Farrakhan and other members of the Nation who knew Malcolm. Since Malcolm's assassination in 1965 the word on the streets of black America had been that Farrakhan was "all up in that." In 1966 three black Muslims were convicted of Malcolm's murder and sentenced to life imprisonment. (As well, many supporters of Malcolm have implicated not only the Nation in the assassination but the Central Intelligence Agency and the Federal Bureau of Investigation.) Farrakhan had been Malcolm's protégé. When Malcolm broke with Elijah Muhammad, the head of the Nation, Farrakhan remained faithful to the Nation. After Malcolm's death, Farrakhan emerged as a black orator and leader who rattled Jewish groups, whites, and conservative blacks. He preached the politics of self-reliance. Many

Americans accused him of racism. They said he was anti-Semitic and inspired ghetto blacks to hate. In 1995 Farrakhan convened the Million Man March in Washington, D.C. The gathering was the largest of its kind in U.S. history.

Lee's relationship with the Nation of Islam preceded his meeting with Minister Farrakhan. The Fruit of Islam (FOI), the Nation's security forces, had secured areas for location shooting during production of *Do the Right Thing* and *Jungle Fever.* FOI cleared drug dealers and crack houses off the block within a matter of forty-eight hours. The decision to continue the relationship between Forty Acres and the FOI with *Malcolm X* rested with Minister Farrakhan.

With great anticipation Lee, accompanied by Malcolm's daughter, Gamilah, flew to Chicago on July 25, 1990, to interview Minister Farrakhan. The ground rules that Farrakhan set for their meeting were simple. He would answer all questions that Lee would ask. Farrakhan's primary concern was that the film not damage the reputation of the Honorable Elijah Muhammad. Farrakhan warned Lee not to be a pawn of Hollywood. In his diary of the meeting Lee wrote:

> [Farrakhan] "…it's been twenty years trying to put this movie out and it hasn't happened yet. It's going to happen because they want it to happen today."
>
> [Lee] "Who's they?"
>
> [Farrakhan] "I'm saying that because white folk have studied you, they know you got courage. They know you love truth and want to make a movie of truth, and I admire that in you too. Now, what is truth, good man? I don't know how much truth you can tell in three hours, or whatever your plan is. But I'm telling you I believe Malcolm X's life is the most exemplary life of the century." [31]

"No white director in the world would have that kind of access," Lee said. "Minister Farrakhan would not have invited Norman Jewison to his house to sit down and tell him about Malcolm because black folks, we just don't trust white folks. And we'd distrust what a white director was going to do with the film. I don't really want to make this a black and white thing…but this is America."[32]

The biggest challenge for Lee was to present Malcolm as a full human being. In the nearly thirty years following his death, Malcolm had become a cultural icon. He was hailed as the epitome of black manhood, along with Kwame Nkrumah, the former president of Ghana, which was the first African nation to gain its independence, in 1960; Bob Marley, the reggae singer; and Marcus Garvey. By the early 1990s, Malcolm was ranked among the visionaries of the black world. Politicians, students, and working-class blacks everywhere still debated his philosophies. Tapes of his speeches were available and sold by street vendors and in bookstores in black communities from Harlem, U.S.A., to Lagos, Nigeria. Lee acknowledged:

> Malcolm meant so much to so many people. He has achieved sainthood. Just like everybody has their own personal relationship with God, a lot of people have their own personal relationship with Malcolm. My challenge was to show his greatness and his humanity. Malcolm loved to laugh. That is something you never got from the media. His sisters and brothers told me all kinds of anecdotes. We couldn't have him ranting and raving the whole movie about "the white man." He was a human being. He loved his wife. He loved his children. He had an undying love for black people. That's what we wanted to show. We didn't want him to be some mythic, god-like, Christ-like figure who was above everybody else.[33]

Artistic control and historical accuracy were just two of the challenges. Seemingly from left field, Lee's politics were challenged. A small but vocal band of black nationalists insinuated that Lee would treat Malcolm's life with the folly of *She's Gotta Have It* or *School Daze*. In essence, there was a backlash against the movie *Malcolm X* before filming even began. Poet Amiri Baraka was among Lee's toughest critics. He predicted that Lee would focus on Malcolm's years as a pimp and his relationships with white women. (Ironically, during the 1960s, Baraka, then known as LeRoi Jones, was himself married to a white woman and followed a lifestyle that Malcolm disapproved of.) "We will not let Malcolm's life be trashed to make middle-class Negroes sleep easier," Baraka vowed.[34]

Lee was unfazed. "I've always understood from the get-go that you cannot please everybody," he responded. "But if people are going to make an intelligent judgment on my film, let it be based on intelligence. Nobody's seen the film." Then in typical Spike Lee/Mars Blackmon style he added: "So they should just shut the f—k up until the movie comes out."[35]

Lee's response did not stop there. Never shy about exposing contradictions and hypocrisy in black America, he asked, "Where were their cries of protest when Norman Jewison was going to do the film? They didn't say a goddamned thing." Lee vowed to remain faithful to the record in *The Autobiography of Malcolm X* as told to Alex Haley. "If Malcolm didn't want people to know certain things, he never would have told that s—t to Alex Haley in the first place," Lee reasoned. [36]

UPHOLDING MALCOLM'S PRODUCTION VALUES

during the film's production the studio balked at Lee's insistence on filming key scenes at Mecca and in Africa. Years before, according to Lee, James Baldwin, who had written the early draft of the script, recalled a memo from a white studio boss advising him to avoid suggesting that Malcolm's trip to Mecca "could have had any political implications, or repercussions."[37] In fact, Malcolm's pilgrimage to Mecca, the holy city of Islam, transformed him from a separatist into an advocate of human rights for all people. During the trip he was trailed by agents of the Federal Bureau of Investigation. On the big screen a sequence of Malcolm in Mecca would be stunning. Lee refused to compromise. The studio suggested that he film the scenes on a beach in New Jersey. It was January 1991, in the dead of winter. Lee refused. He also turned down the suggestion that the filming of these scenes be moved to Arizona. He pointed out that the state of Arizona does not celebrate the birthday of Dr. Martin Luther King, Jr. He would not spend two cents of his budget in the desert there. Besides, the Sahara, where Mecca is located, didn't have pitchfork cactus or tumbleweed.

The studio threatened to shut down production. Lee needed more money. He recalled lying in bed and remembering Malcolm's message. "Malcolm always preached self-reliance," Lee said. "I didn't have to sit around begging the studio to give me anything. Other films didn't get this nickel-and-dime treatment." [38] A speech that Malcolm delivered in 1963 was particularly inspiring as the production stood at this crossroads:

> The white man wants you to remain a boy, he wants you to remain a lackey, he wants you to remain dependent on him, wants you to come looking to him for some kind of advice, some kind of teaching. No. You teach yourself, and stand up for yourself, and respect yourself, and know yourself, and defend yourself, and be yourself and you will be recognized as an intelligent person. [39]

To complete the film, Lee returned to guerrilla financing, but on a much larger scale. Lee needed big money, and he knew exactly where he should get it. He was about to pull off the finest display of self-reliance that African American entertainment had ever seen. Bill Cosby, Michael Jordan, Oprah Winfrey, Magic Johnson, Prince, Janet Jackson, Tracy Chapman, and other prominent African Americans in sports and entertainment gave Lee the funds to complete the work. Lee's strategy was perfect.

The film executives at Warner Brothers had no idea where Lee's money was coming from. But on May 19, 1992, Malcolm's sixty-seventh birthday, they found out. Lee held a press conference at the Schomburg Center for Research in Black Culture in Harlem. The center, a special branch of the New York Public Library, is considered the foremost archive of material on the African American community. The remains of Langston Hughes are interred there.

Lee, with Dr. Betty Shabazz by his side, told the world how he got the money to continue work on *Malcolm X*.

David Du Bois, the son of W. E. B. Du Bois, had cautioned Lee that he was playing with dynamite. "They don't want this," Du Bois, a college professor at the University of Ghana said. "Any leader who starts to talk about Africa, and African Americans, watch out."[40]

The final cut (or version) of the film ran nearly four hours. Lee chastised anyone who suggested that filmgoers would not sit through the epic, which had no intermission. He contended that Malcolm's life had the same magnitude as that of Mahatma Gandhi, the Indian human-rights activist who led his countrymen in nonviolent protest against British colonialism. Sir Richard Attenborough's epic film *Gandhi* ran just over three hours. Few critics balked at its length. Likewise, Francis Ford Coppola's Mafia chronicle *The Godfather,* as well as its sequel, were long films. The sequel ran almost three and a half hours and included a ten-minute intermission. All these films were huge successes. Warner Brothers said that theater owners would not like a long film because that meant that they could not show it as many times in a day. Lee was unmoved. "Malcolm was a man of many truths. In Malcolm's life we see growth. We see movement. We see evolution. His life went from A to Z. You have to take the time to show that evolution and growth and many different lives that Malcolm had."[41]

By the time *Malcolm X* opened on Thanksgiving weekend in 1992, Malcolm's image was everywhere in the media. Several publishing companies produced new works on the author. "I want teachers to take their classes to see this film," Lee said. "This is American history."[42] Lee caused a furor when he suggested that all African Americans take the day off from work or school to attend the film on the Friday after Thanksgiving. He said he was thinking like a businessman. In the movie business the first twelve days of a film's release are the most critical. The box-office receipts, particularly from the first weekend, indicate whether or not the studio will book the movie into more theaters. Lee exposed the inner workings of the film industry. No black filmmaker had ever done that before. "Make it plain" was what Malcolm used to call imparting truth to the public. Lee broke it all the way down.

When the film opened in theaters across America, audiences talked back to the screen. Lee and Denzel Washington had re-created the "call and response" of Malcolm's red-hot orations. "Denzel and I knew we had to make a great picture," Lee remembered. "That's the kind of pressure we were under. We could not go down in history as the guys who messed up Malcolm's life."[43]

The film, which opens with a burning American flag and footage of the Rodney King beating, ends with a message from Nelson Mandela and a classroom of South African school children proclaiming: "I am Malcolm X! I am Malcolm X! I am Malcolm X!" As the credits roll, the faces of the film's superstar saviors appear on the screen. Lee wanted the world to know that he said, "Thank you."

Even as enthusiastic reviews came in, controversy continued. Lee accused theaters, under orders from Warner Brothers, of crediting ticket sales for *Malcolm X* to other features. Many also felt that the Academy of Motion Picture Arts and Sciences should have nominated Lee for Best Director. The omission of Spike Lee in this category was akin to armed robbery, they argued. Denzel Washington told many journalists that racism was at the root of the omission.

CROOKLYN

t he two-year experience of directing *Malcolm X* left Lee exhausted. "I don't want to kill myself making movies," he said.[44] As he approached middle age, Lee decided to take another approach to filmmaking. Following *Malcolm X*, Lee began to produce films as well as direct them. He established a deal with Universal Pictures to bring the works of other African American filmmakers to the screen. (At the same time Lee was free to work on his own projects.) "I can do a whole lot of things at once," he said. [45]

For his seventh film, Lee pitched a curve ball. *Crooklyn* is the story of a summer in the life of a Brooklyn family during the 1970s. It is told from the point of view of Troy, a ten-year-old girl. Some critics applauded the film as being the baby of "a kinder, gentler Spike Lee." Written with his four siblings, this picture was obviously autobiographical.

Lee recalls a time of innocence, when children could be children and a fist fight was a fist fight, not a homicide. With *Crooklyn*, once again, Lee's finger is on black America's pulse. There is a painful sequence of Troy's aunt unbraiding her cornrows and combing out her hair to make it straight. ("I don't know why your mamma put this mess up in your head," her aunt tells her.) As the aunt yanks on Troy's hair and complains that it is not "good hair," moviegoers winced. Likewise, scenes of Troy's brothers having their afro hair-styles "picked" captured the most intimate moments of African American life. Lee insisted that his actors let their hair grow out into afros. He didn't want them wearing wigs. In the 1990s afro wigs had become camp. Lee wanted his movie to be real.

In interviews Lee joked about the challenges of filming a movie with so many child actors. He realized that children could not be directed like adults. They had shorter attention spans and needed to go to the bathroom more frequently. Critics asked Lee if he had gotten "soft" with his success. No, Lee replied. There were many levels of truth, and *Crooklyn* represented his childhood. (Gordon Parks had a similar response to critics who felt that *The Learning Tree* was out of touch with the militancy of the 1960s.) "We do what families do: We fight, yell, hug, and love," said Lee.[46]

THE JACKIE ROBINSON STORY

t he true measure of Lee's power came with the relative ease with which he secured the rights to film *The Jackie Robinson Story*. Documentary filmmaker Ken Burns planned to direct the picture.

Burns had interviewed Rachel Robinson, the widow of the first black man to play in the major leagues, for his 1994 documentary *Baseball*. At the same time, unknown to Mrs. Robinson, Burns was also trying to to secure the rights to direct a screenplay on her husband. He never said one word to her. When she found out, Mrs. Robinson was not pleased. "You would think that while we were sitting and recording for three hours he might have said, 'By the way I'm thinking about doing something on Jack.'"[47]

Nor was Robinson pleased to learn that the screenplay Burns wanted would be told through the eyes of Branch Rickey and Red Barber. Rickey, the general manager of the Brooklyn Dodgers, had brought Robinson into the major leagues. Barber was a baseball broadcaster assigned to cover the Dodgers. Both men were white. Rachel Robinson disapproved of Burns's maneuverings and of the script. So she called Spike Lee. "I still feel that a black man can understand another black man and all the nuances of his life better than anyone else can," Robinson said. "Not that there aren't white writers who have written about blacks. There have been white writers who have written about black people and done a good job. I just think you have an edge when you come out of the same experience."[48]

This time Spike Lee did not have to say a word. He simply stood next to Rachel Robinson at a press conference and smiled the broad smile of a confident man.

● CLOCKERS

In 1995, *Clockers* became one of Lee's most critically acclaimed works. The film is based on a best-selling novel by Richard Price. The movie is the tale of Strike, a young Brooklyn man, who sells drugs or "clocks." When a man is murdered, all logic points to Strike as the prime suspect. Strike's brother, Victor, a hardworking, upstanding, earnest citizen, confesses to the murders, however. A persistent cop refuses to accept Victor's confession and Strike's blasé, ghetto-cool denial.

This tense urban drama was universally hailed by critics. They called *Clockers* his best work to date. Lee said the film represented the first "joint" in which whites did not feel that he pointed the finger of blame for the chaotic conditions of America's inner cities at white America, and so he dismissed the praise that white film reviewers lavished on him. *Malcolm X*, he maintained, was his tour de force.

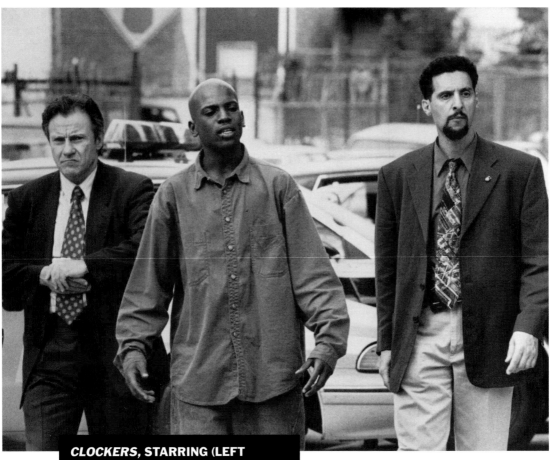

CLOCKERS, STARRING (LEFT TO RIGHT) HARVEY KEITEL, MEKHI PHIFER, AND JOHN TURTURRO, RECEIVED CRITICAL ACCLAIM.

FIVE
Created in Their Own Image

When Spike Lee elbowed his way into Hollywood, he set the stage for many African American filmmakers to present a wide range of cinematic visions. Upon his first success, the press began to clamor for "the next Spike Lee." But there was no next Spike Lee. Instead, there was an entirely new film movement. After *She's Gotta Have It,* Hollywood rediscovered that African Americans have interesting stories to tell—and make box-office profits. It was the same lesson that Hollywood had begrudgingly learned from race movies and blaxploitation films.

In the 1990s some of the stories of black filmmakers fit neatly into Hollywood formulas. They became very successful within the Hollywood system. Their stories were "packaged" by Hollywood executives. These businessmen were interested in reaching the widest possible audience. Often the cultural content of their films was low or nonexistent. They were packed with sex and violence.

But there was another kind of filmmaker, those who were not dazzled by Hollywood dreams. Such filmmakers saw themselves as cultural workers. They made movies for an audience that was generally more sophisticated and appreciative of complex story lines and multidimensional characters. These filmmakers were dedicated to creating more new images of African Americans in movies. Like Lee, they were willing to do so without the backing of the industry, "the plantation."

To many, their advent held the promise of a new understanding. "Black people know everything about white people," Spike Lee told a documentary film crew. "From the time we can think, that's all we see on TV, on the radio, magazines, movies. We are bombarded with white folks. Conversely, white Americans know very little about African Americans." [1]

THE DROP SQUAD
DELIVERS A MESSAGE

butch Robinson and David Johnson were inspired by Lee's example. Both came from broadcast-news backgrounds and wanted to do more. Then they saw *She's Gotta Have It*. "We can't give Spike Lee enough credit. Before Spike, there was really no one of our age group who was making films," Butch recalled. "When I saw his first film, I knew that I could make my own movie." [2]

Robinson and Johnson produced a "short" (a mini-preview of what the filmmakers hope will eventually become a feature-length work) called *The Session*, based on a short story by David Taylor. The pair got to know Lee when they worked on the crew of *Do the Right Thing*. A few years later they screened *The Session* for Lee, who liked what he saw. "It was an original script, it was topical and they were excellent filmmakers," Lee said of the short, which was eventually renamed *The DROP Squad*. "*DROP Squad* was different and we need diversity in [film] subject matter. If our film was going to be true to our culture and be entertaining, we had to reflect present themes," said Lee. [3]

DAVID JOHNSON, DIRECTOR AND CO-WRITER, ON THE SET OF *THE DROP SQUAD*, WHICH WAS PRODUCED BY SPIKE LEE.

Lee was in a position to offer the brothers a deal. Through an agreement with Universal Pictures, Lee would choose, executive-produce, and oversee the budget of select films by new directors. He said that stepping down from the director's chair for some projects would allow him to have even more influence. He chose to help develop *The DROP Squad.* (In 1994 he also served as executive producer for *Tales from the Hood,* a horror flick.)

The DROP Squad is about the deprogramming of African Americans who have sold out. "DROP" stands for Deprogramming and Restoration of Pride. The DROP Squad is a group of underground militants. They kidnap people who have gotten "too far out of line." Drug dealers, wayward preachers, black actresses who wear blue contact lenses, and buppies are all prime candidates for the group's radical mission.

"There's no way I could have sold my film to Hollywood," Butch Robinson says. "They wouldn't understand. Spike understood immediately. He knew what we were trying to do. This is a film about 1990s black radicals who take things into their own hands." [4]

Bruford Jamison, Jr., is a buppie who works in a large advertising agency concocting campaigns that are offensive to African Americans. His big accounts are Mumblin' Jack Malt Liquor ("Available everywhere black people are served") and Gospel Pak Chicken ("Eating chicken this good is like dying and going to heaven," says one TV commercial character, an overweight choir woman in a blinding purple robe. "It sho' is," replies her friend. "Now you can have your piece on earth."). [5]

Bruford's co-workers and family object to this work, but Bruford dismisses them. He sees nothing wrong with these characterizations. After all, he is moving up the corporate ladder. Bruford has "gone Hollywood" and distanced himself from his cousins Stink and the irresponsible Flip. Tensions arise within the Jamison family when Bruford refuses to help Flip get a job in his firm's mailroom. Someone asks Bruford if he's still black.

"There are so many arguments about what it means to be African American," observed Shelby Stone, who co-produced the film with Robinson. "It gets so tricky because who gets to determine what is the correct way to be black?" [6] This serious issue within the African American community could not be confronted by a white filmmaker.

Bruford's family grows disgusted with him, and Bruford's sister Lenora calls the DROP Squad. Bruford is snatched off the street. He resists his reprogramming. Only when his cousin Flip appears at the DROP Squad boot camp does Bruford realize what a sellout he has been.

Robinson, Taylor, Lee, and Stone did not have a wide audience in mind as they worked on the film. "This is not a hip-hop film," Robinson explained. "This is not necessarily a film for young people. This is a film for black folks who work for white people, and who understand the racial dynamics of their relationship with whites. This is a film for people who know what it's like to have your morals messed with and to have your ideas stolen." [7]

The DROP Squad clearly packed a moral message. By the end of the film Bruford has resigned from the advertising agency where he worked and opened up his own business. The rejection of the white world was still something new in black films. Situated in the ghetto, this story portrayed African Americans who rarely ventured outside of their community. To see middle-class blacks kidnapped off the streets and forced to examine their lifestyles was quite radical. "This is a satire," Robinson said. "In Hollywood, black people aren't allowed to make satire. That's the trick bag that black filmmakers are put in. There is an audience that is wider than gangster shoot-'em-up films. This is outrageous satire."[8]

ROBERT TOWNSEND BREAKS OUT

as an African American in Hollywood, Robert Townsend knew about outrageous and ridiculous situations. At times it seemed as if his life were a satire on trying to make it as a Hollywood actor. White producers offered him steady work playing pimps, pushers, slaves, and other lowlife characters. Townsend was praying for a dramatic role that would give his career dignity. So was every other black actor in Hollywood.

Finally, he decided to write and direct his own movies. His first effort was *Hollywood Shuffle*. The film is a satire about the racism that has dogged blacks in Hollywood since the 1903 debut of *Uncle Tom's Cabin*. Townsend's film, in which he plays an actor named Bobby, closely mirrors his career. The range of roles open to him is very limited. His only options are to sell his soul and play pimps, drug addicts, or thieves, or to slave as a busboy at Winky-Dinky Dog, a miserable little dead-end job at a hot-dog stand. "*Hollywood Shuffle* was borne out of a lot of pain," Townsend admitted. "I pointed out how ridiculous the film industry really is."[9]

Townsend produced *Hollywood Shuffle* on a shoestring budget, in much the same manner that Spike Lee produced *She's Gotta Have It*. He ran all of his credit cards to the limit and then borrowed from friends.

Townsend would be the first black director to bring satire to the big screen. His friend Keenan Ivory Wayans produced *I'm Gonna Git You Sucka,* a hilarious spoof on the blaxploitation films. Isaac Hayes, Jim Brown, and Bernie Casey, all major stars from the blaxploitation era, were reunited on the screen for this picture. Although neither of these movies was a "serious film," they showed that blacks in Hollywood could actually laugh at their situation, and they did not have to do so in a manner that was degrading. At the same time, the films underscored the need for black determination.

"If you are black and want to get something done," Townsend said, "you will have to go down a different avenue." [10] Like Micheaux, Townsend knew how to cut corners when he was filming. "If I write a 20 million dollar movie and I don't have the money to make it with, that's stupid. I have to make a script that's going to be something I can afford to shoot. If I want a car crash, but I can't afford to stage a car crash, I'll go for some makeup. I'll make a guy look bloody, like he just got out of a car crash. Sometimes you have to adapt to the conditions." [11]

Townsend hoped his satire would prompt black actors in Hollywood to give more thought to the types of roles they play. "If I play a pimp in a movie and the next time they offer me a pimp, they're going to say, 'Robert, you did it once, you've got to do it again.' If I play a slave, they say, 'Hey, you cried once and got whipped, you can cry again and get whipped'. If you do bulls—t, then you get known for bulls—t. If I did that degrading Stepin Fetchit shuffling kind of stuff, I couldn't face my family and friends. There's no pride in that." [12]

Many actors said that they took whatever roles were offered them in the hopes that something better would come along. This argument had been heard before in the days of Hattie McDaniel and Stepin Fetchit. However, there was a big difference. Now there were plenty of African American filmmakers. It became easier for actors to say no to roles they found demeaning. Cuba Gooding, Jr., the star of John Singleton's *Boyz N the Hood,* pointed out that there was to be a method to the madness. In fact, he knew Singleton because they had both been on the "pimps and slaves circuit." "The reality is that you've got to eat.

I've done a lot of television. I did some rotten roles. Pimps, pushers. They didn't have nothing positive to say. My whole motive was to put myself in a position where I may be able to change things. I got the opportunity for *Boyz N the Hood* because I was around. John Singleton remembered me from doing all the bad stuff. He knew I was a good actor."[13]

YOUNG, BLACK, AND CONFRONTATIONAL

among the most successful films by young black filmmakers have been those in the *Boyz N the Hood* genre. John Singleton's 1991 tale of gang life in the Compton section of Los Angeles held the nation spellbound. Cuba Gooding, Jr., starred as Tre, a bright teenager raised by a loving father, played by Laurence Fishburne. (Many single African American women called Fishburne's character the ghetto dream dad.) Singleton contrasts Tre's way, thanks to his father's strong presence, of negotiating the deadly streets with the short-tempered and often fatal methods of his best friends. Doughboy, played by rapper Ice Cube, is a jobless young brother who has done time in jail and seems destined to die young. But he is more than a hoodlum. Singleton looks with understanding into Doughboy's troubled soul.

Boyz N the Hood was nominated for two Academy Awards, Best Screenplay and Best Director. Singleton was the youngest director ever to be nominated for this prize. Many blacks in Hollywood believed that Singleton was handpicked by his Hollywood studio to be "the next Spike Lee." Singleton himself admitted his debt to Lee. With his success, one critic noted that Singleton became "the sellable black male commodity [Hollywood] privately hoped for, namely an easier-to-deal-with Spike Lee."[14]

Singleton's second film was *Poetic Justice*, a love story starring Janet Jackson and Tupac Shakur. Jackson plays Justice, a tormented young hairdresser, and Shakur is Lucky, a hardworking young postman. Singleton's third film, *Higher Learning*, deals with the freshman year of three college students on an integrated campus. In this film, Singleton explores the politics of race on a college campus, mirroring the tense relations that existed between blacks and whites in many integrated schools. The film also explores the identity crisis of black collegiates, which Spike Lee had also addressed in his film *School Daze* several years earlier.

Just as a rash of blaxploitation films followed *Shaft* and *Superfly* in the 1970s, several films that were similar to *Boyz N the Hood* flooded theaters in the 1990s. The formula for these films went like this: Angry young black men, trapped in the ghetto, try to kill or not be killed by other angry young black men. At least one of them has done time. At least one other is committed to escaping his ghetto life. The story is almost always backed with a funky, "phat" rap soundtrack.

JOHN SINGLETON, DIRECTOR OF THE 1991 FILM *BOYZ N THE HOOD*, WAS THE YOUNGEST DIRECTOR EVER TO BE NOMINATED FOR AN ACADEMY AWARD.

SCENE FROM SINGLETON'S
THIRD FILM, *HIGHER LEARNING*,
STARRING LAURENCE FISHBURNE AND OMAR EPPS.

Some of these films, however, were not formulaic—for example, *Straight Out of Brooklyn*, directed by 19-year-old Matty Rich; *Juice*, directed by Ernest Dickerson, the much-lauded cinematographer of Spike Lee's early joints; and *Menace II Society*, directed by the Hughes Brothers. Each film documented the senseless black-on-black violence that plagues communities from South Central Los Angeles to Brooklyn, New York. Each was critically acclaimed, and theaters had trouble handling the crowds. The relevancy of the films became clear when shooting and other violence occurred in the movies houses showing them.

Particularly powerful was *Menace II Society*. The Hughes Brothers, with several hip-hop videos to their credit, made a hard-hitting film. *Movieline* magazine noted that *Menace* "embodied everything that is frightening and out-of-control in our cities."[15] The film's main character, O-Dog, describes himself as "The craziest nigger alive, America's nightmare: young, black and doesn't give a f—k."[16] The plot features plenty of violence and profanity. Some found it depressing, some found it intriguing. It was, without a doubt, disturbing.

Dead Presidents was a sophomoric feature-film outing for the Hughes brothers. In this tense drama set in the 1970s, Larenze Tate, who starred in Matty Rich's second film, *The Inkwell*, plays a Vietnam veteran. After serving a bloody tour of duty, the vet, Anthony Curtis, returns to his hometown, the Bronx, to find that his war-hero celebrity status fades fast because he has no real skills. The armed forces turned him into a killing machine, and little else. As he struggles to make ends meet and provide for his family, the promise of a stable future cruelly escapes him. Frustration, the Black Power movement, and pride combine to pressure Curtis to mastermind the heist of an armored truck headed for the Federal Reserve to burn old money, or "dead presidents." With this film the Hughes Brothers displayed a highly stylized form of filmmaking that reflected elements from Japanese kabuki theater, complete with dramatic makeup.

On a grander scale is *New Jack City*, directed by Mario Van Peebles, the son of Melvin Van Peebles. The film is a forceful drama about a ruthless crack

CO-PRODUCERS, CO-DIRECTORS, AND TWIN BROTHERS ALLEN AND ALBERT HUGHES, ON LOCATION FILMING *DEAD PRESIDENTS*. THEY CREATED THEIR FIRST CRITICALLY ACCLAIMED FILM *MENACE II SOCIETY* WHEN THEY WERE TWENTY YEARS OLD.

cocaine kingpin, Nino Barnes, played by Wesley Snipes, and based on the true-life story of Leroy "Nicky" Barnes. Snipes is diabolical in his portrayal of the ruthless Barnes, a legend on the Harlem streets. Nothing matters to Barnes. He laughs at the law. He wouldn't hesitate to use a child as a decoy during a shoot-out. He assaults old men. He steals his main man's girlfriend. Rapper Ice-T plays the good cop who is determined to put Barnes behind bars.

Young urban moviegoers were drawn to the film. *New Jack City* was one of the biggest-grossing black films in history. The film's title was coined by writer Barry Michael Cooper to describe the new attitude of masculinity in the African American community. But many saw the revenues that come from films like *New Jack City* as blood money. The feeling was that such films exploited the degradation of African Americans in inner cities. Leaders in the black community and free-speech advocates debated whether such images needed to be created at all. Minister Louis Farrakhan maintained that the real reason *Menace II Society* was so disturbing to America was that it exposed the awful results of America's hypocrisy. He said that street hoodlums were merely following in the footsteps of white American males. "If these [young inner city African American males] are menace number two, who do you think is menace one?" the outspoken minister rhetorically asked. [17]

The audience that Van Peebles drew comprised more than matinee rowdies. Many of them were straight-up gangsters aspiring to be on the big screen like Nicky Barnes. Within Hollywood, many blacks had harsh words for such films. "Suddenly, anybody who falls out of a housing project or a low-riding car is getting a studio deal," actress Alfre Woodard observed. "I resent these movies being passed off as cinema." She urged young filmmakers to look beyond the millions of dollars that studios were offering them to make such pictures. "The conditions of these movie deals have nothing to do with African Americans as people." [18] She herself frequently turned down roles that she considered derogatory.

Actress Halle Berry, who was directed by the Hudlins and Spike Lee, was of the same mind. "*New Jack City* and *Juice* are a part of our story. *Boyz N the Hood* was a wonderful story that needed to be made, but we need to get away from that. We have so many stories to tell. We need to tell stories that are going to advance our race, not keep us in the middle of drugs and violence." [19]

Woodard and Berry were not the only actors who were skeptical of what the mainstream perceived as so-called progress in black films. "I'm frustrated," said Natalie Oliver, one of Denzel Washington's co-stars in *Mississippi Masala*.

There are not a lot of roles for black actresses. Halle Berry gets all the roles for pretty girls. Angela Basset gets the dramatic roles, and then there's Whoopi Goldberg. The rest of us deal with table scraps. I am not all that impressed with the emerging young filmmakers. A lot of the young men who are emerging are talented but they are professional amateurs, so to speak. They present hardcore images that don't need to be perpetuated. Do we need to see more movies with black men killing each other? Is that the kind of film that our producers and directors should be making? I understand they are doing what the market will bear. But where do we draw the line?[20]

In an earlier era, actors would not have demanded better roles in such a public manner, but the times were changing.

ANOTHER SIDE OF VAN PEEBLES

f or his part, Mario Van Peebles showed he could make movies about more than gangsters. After *New Jack City* came *Posse*. Set during the Spanish-American War (1892), Posse is the story of freedmen who establish settlements in the West. Part *Bronze Buckaroo* (from the days of race films) and part *Buck and the Preacher*, Posse is educational and entertaining. Speaking directly to his audience, Van Peebles opens the film with the following words: "Although ignored by Hollywood and most history books, the memory of more than eight thousand black cowboys that roamed in the early west still lives on."[21]

The film centers on conflicts stemming from the "grandfather clause," which stated that if a black man's grandfather had not voted before 1867, he could not vote. Local governments took this a step further. They used it as a basis for seizing what little property the freedmen had acquired. The film shows how the freedmen responded to the hooded nightriders who burned churches and schools. Native Americans are presented not as scalp-hunting savages but as allies to the black frontiersmen.

MARIO VAN PEEBLES
DIRECTED AND STARRED IN *POSSE*, AMONG THE FIRST FILMS
TO REFLECT THE MULTIRACIAL CHARACTER OF THE WEST

Van Peebles had to fight to make his film. "I was teased and laughed at for wanting to make *Posse*," he told a group of students at Texas Southern University. "To them [white male studio executives] black cowboys didn't exist." But Van Peebles clearly liked sitting in the director's chair. "I'm probably attracted to directing because of the power. As an actor, my responsibility is to the character, the characters I interface with, and to learn my own set of lines. As director, you're not worried about yourself. You're worried about the whole damn thing—what lens to use, everybody's lines, close-ups, what colors to use, everything. But along with those responsibilities, there's a certain amount of freedom and the ability to send a message."[22]

STRAIGHT OUT OF EAST ST. LOUIS: THE HUDLIN BROTHERS

When Yale film student Warrington Hudlin decided that he wanted to be a filmmaker, he knew he'd have to build a support system. In 1978 he founded the Black Filmmakers Foundation (BFF). BFF represented a generation of blacks who were knowledgeable in the history, art, economics, and politics of filmmaking. Hudlin and his colleagues realized that Hollywood usually set the standards of taste for moviegoers. A lot of good films by African Americans were not getting made because they lacked studio support. Hudlin wanted to educate black moviegoers. "The public needs to understand that what makes a film black is who is behind the camera, not who is in front of the camera," Hudlin preached. Hudlin believed in the self-reliance philosophies of Malcolm X and Marcus Garvey. "The long-term goal is that we should establish our own independent mechanism. We need to identify our markets, and produce films for that market."[23]

Along with his brother Reginald, a director, Hudlin would make *House Party* and *Boomerang*. *House Party* is about a group of friends who break a weeknight curfew to attend a party. The film is based on Reginald Hudlin's senior project at Harvard University, which won a student Academy Award.

The Hudlin Brothers come from East St. Louis, Missouri, and they made sure that Hollywood knew they had a different sensibility. (Many African Americans affectionately call East St. Louis, a city of rib joints and blues clubs, "the blackest city in the country.") "Most black films are shot in Los Angeles or Harlem," Reginald Hudlin noted. "But there's a whole lot of black life that falls in the middle. I wanted to shoot a film that captures the life of those neighborhoods. *House Party* is important because it portrays black teenagers as fully developed characters, not stereotypes."[24]

Among the cast are comedians Martin Lawrence and Robin Harris, and the rap duo Kid 'N' Play. As Play's father, Harris portrays a hardworking, "take-no-mess" single father to a tee. In one scene he tells his still-sleeping son to go downstairs and eat "some of the s—t I fixed for you." The son protests the use of profanity. Then, when he goes downstairs, he beholds a deluxe breakfast of pancakes, omelets, cereal, and sausage. His dad's love is evident. The Hudlins captured the rough-handed tenderness of so many African American fathers from the Midwest. When Harris tells his son, "I don't care if Marvin Gaye is going to be at that party, you'd better not be there," he is again referring to contemporary black culture.[25] "We had to fight to keep something as simple as that Marvin Gaye line in," Warrington remembered. "The attitude of the studio was that Marvin Gaye was dead, so what was the point."[26] To Hudlin, the executives didn't get it. Marvin Gaye is one of the most beloved singers in black America. His records and his image endure. The Marvin Gaye comment went over the heads of white studio executives, but African Americans certainly got it.

JACKSON-McHENRY'S ART OF THE DEAL

hollywood's new African American community had a distinct edge over blacks who had worked in Tinseltown years before. As Sidney Poitier predicted, more blacks were learning the business of making movies. A few set up their own production companies. They became allies with studio executives who were able to approve, or "green-light," a picture.

Two of the sharpest African American entrepreneurs in Hollywood were George Jackson and Doug McHenry. The partners had learned thoroughly the inner workings of Hollywood. The Jackson-McHenry company produced *New Jack City, Jason's Lyric, A Rage in Harlem,* and *House Party II.* Jackson and McHenry built a reputation as determined streetwise producers. They took chances. Both had come up through the ranks of the studio systems. Jackson was a Harvard graduate. Along with Robert Townsend, he had worked at Richard Pryor's short-lived Indigo films.

In terms of box-office success, the Jackson-McHenry movies made more money than films like *She's Gotta Have It* or *Hollywood Shuffle.* Many of their movies were pitched at a hard-edged urban audience. When *New Jack City* was released in 1991, there was not much difference between what was on the screen and what was in the streets, or in the theater, for that matter. Violence erupted in movie houses across the country. "The same attitudes and conflicts that exist outside are brought inside," journalist Nelson George wrote. "In many cases these shootings would have happened somewhere else—it just happened that the film's appeal too often placed enemies in violent proximity." [27]

Jackson and McHenry responded by bringing more African Americans into the film industry. In 1992, with BFF and the American Film Institute, the pair put together a conference in Los Angeles entitled "Breaking the Cycle: The Business of African American Filmmaking in the 90s."

Devil in a Blue Dress was director Carl Franklin's foray into period film-making. Set in Los Angeles in the late 1940s, this whodunit was based on a novel from the best-selling series by mystery writer Walter Mosley. Denzel Washington, a matinee monarch in the tradition of Sidney Poitier and Harry Belafonte, with a dry wit and suave swagger played private detective Ezekiel "Easy" Rawlings. *Devil in a Blue Dress* transcended the lighthearted comic-book camp of Bill Duke's *A Rage in Harlem.* But *Devil* still had many side-splitting moments, provided by Don Cheadle in the supporting role of Mouse, Easy's trigger-happy sidekick.

Devil represented a bona fide big-budget period piece—the kind that aspiring filmmaker Preston Whitmore was told that Hollywood would never support. The fact that Denzel Washington, one of Hollywood's top leading men, could acquire the rights to make the movie, indicated a level of black clout in Hollywood.

PRESTON WHITMORE'S HOLLYWOOD EDUCATION

One of the newcomers to Hollywood who clearly learned the movie business before making a film was Preston Whitmore. After an honorable discharge from the Marines in 1986, Whitmore, a native Detroiter who joined the service to escape a dead-end life and a broken heart, settled in Los Angeles. During his time in the service he began to write. Working as a security guard at an exclusive Hollywood high rise, Whitmore was soon befriended by many major figures in the film industry. He began writing screenplays. "I wrote fast. I wrote quick," Whitmore said. " I knew that you had to grab your reader within the first ten pages of a script. These executives were reading an average of fifty scripts a week. I always asked myself, what could I do to make my work special? These people, who were becoming my friends, were only too happy to read my work." [28]

The consensus was that Whitmore was indeed a man who could build a very lucrative career. There was just one not-so-small problem. Whitmore's forte was period pieces. "I ended up writing what I thought was going to be a sure shot. I wrote a script called *No Reply*." [29] This was a thriller set in Detroit during World War II. A soldier returns home to find his brother embroiled in an organized-crime ring. "I really poured my blood into that screenplay. The only problem was that I didn't know that Hollywood wasn't making black period pieces. This was an epic. It would have cost $20 million to make this film. They read my stuff, their attitude was 'Boy, you got talent. But we can't sell none of this.'" [30]

Whitmore was disappointed, but he began to study what Hollywood was buying. He became a writer for hire. Producers would call him with ideas and he would produce a script. Or else he would be called in to "doctor" a script that wasn't working out. "I learned pretty quickly that it's easier to make money in Hollywood than it is to make a picture." [31] Somehow his deals always seemed to fall through. It was getting depressing. Finally he hooked up with Doug McHenry and George Jackson.

Over a series of long lunches in expensive restaurants, the partners gave Preston the lowdown on Hollywood. "They'd be sitting there in these fantastic restaurants smoking these big stogy cigars. They'd go through every appetizer on the menu. They'd order drinks. Whenever they talked to me, they always came with a check for my services." Whitmore left those lunches knowing what top brass were thinking. "I was getting a quick education in development. I learned what the studios looked at, and how they developed characters. What made them make a movie." [32]

Eventually Whitmore took a project to McHenry and Jackson, *The Walking Dead.* It is the story of four soldiers in Vietnam in 1972 on their last mission. As they negotiate the terrain, there are flashbacks (or "back stories," to use film terminology) of each man's life. As a former Marine, Whitmore knew the language of war and the dynamics of combat. "Although there have been numerous films on Vietnam, such as *Born on the 4th of July* and *Platoon,* none of them [has] been from a black perspective."[33] Working with an agent, Whitmore began shopping the script around. McHenry and Jackson were interested, but they were busy with preproduction for *Jason's Lyric,* an urban love story that takes place in Houston's notorious Fifth Ward.

Past experiences had taught Whitmore that he needed to secure a commitment for the script while it was hot. He decided that he would direct it himself. "Arsenio Hall, Spike Lee, and Denzel Washington were all interested in this script. But they didn't want me to direct." Whitmore held his ground. Savoy Pictures gave him a shoestring budget and thirty-six days to shoot the film in Florida. "I was a lunatic," he recalled.[34]

Whitmore pointed out that his film fell into the genre of an action thriller. He was not looking to change the world with *The Walking Dead.* "At the same time the film is not a B-grade movie like *Rambo.* It is more than blood and guts. It is a serious drama. We look at everyday guys who are standing at the crossroads of their lives. Everybody doesn't make it back from the mission. I learned in the service that people have all kinds of motivations for why they are there. Most of it has very little to do with patriotism."[35]

Although his film is about war, Whitmore claims that there is a higher message in *The Walking Dead.* "The image of the African American male right now is that you are either a gangster, a rapper, or a basketball player. That's the only way you can be a hero. The only time you see African American males with weapons in the movies, they are gangsters. They are destroying each other. Here are guys that are heroes."[36]

Ultimately, Whitmore said he moved comfortably within the system. "I know what Hollywood wants."[37]

LESLIE HARRIS PRODUCES TRUTH 24 FPS

there was at least one group of African American filmmakers who also knew what Hollywood wanted but refused to produce it. They were African American female directors. The overwhelming majority of commercial African American filmmakers have been male. Most female directors had produced either documentaries or intellectual and cultural films shown at small art-house theaters on college campuses, at museums, or in bohemian haunts like Greenwich Village in New York City.

With *Just Another Girl on the IRT*, in 1993, Leslie Harris became the first African American female director to have a feature film with major distribution. Harris was not based in Hollywood. She lived in New York and belonged to the BFF. When her money ran low, she received grant money and assistance to complete her film from writer Nelson George, an early Spike Lee supporter, and novelist Terry McMillan.

Her movie captures the tensions in the life of a high school junior, Chantel, who becomes pregnant. With her heart set on becoming a doctor, Chantel successfully conceals her pregnancy from her parents. Throughout her ordeal Chantel continues to study hard and get good grades. Yet for all of her academic discipline, Chantel is immature when it comes to deciding about her pregnancy. She goes on a shopping spree with money that her boyfriend, Tyrone, has given her for an abortion. To conceal her weight gain from her parents, Chantel buys her clothing in two sizes, wearing and washing the larger ones herself, while putting her regular-size clothes into the laundry her mother does. The inspiration for the film came from conversations that Harris overheard as she took the bus or the subway in New York City. "These young ladies had some amazing stories to tell. I had never seen their stories on screen." [38]

Harris produced the film through her production company, Truth 24 FPS (frames per second). "The film goes through the camera twenty-four frames

per second," Harris explained, "and I thought it was very important to make images that were very truthful on screen."[39] Harris maintained innocence and hope in all of her characters. She refused to present stereotypes. Tyrone drives a jeep that his mother bought him. He is a spoiled mama's boy, not a gangster. Chantel's parents are hardworking people. There are no drugs, domestic violence, illiteracy, or crime in her life. Harris observed:

> In a lot of so-called 'new jack' films teenagers come across acting as adults. I wanted to show the story of a seventeen-year-old girl who was facing a problem she's never faced before. Teen pregnancy didn't surprise me, but it surprises people who don't live in the African American community. Many people don't know how intelligent these young kids are. They are perceptive, ambitious and driven. Pregnancy was not the end of Chantel's life. That's what I wanted to show.[40]

Some potential investors suggested that Harris "color" the script to make it more attractive to Hollywood. "I was asked to make Chantel's boyfriend a drug dealer. They asked me to take the parents out. I refused."[41] To tell such a story Harris knew that she would have to make it on her own. She shot the movie in seventeen days.

Harris fell in love with films growing up in Cleveland. A creative child, she always lived on the artistic fringe. She used to show movies on her bedroom wall. "We didn't have enough money to buy a screen, so I used a sheet. I was fascinated with the moving images. Charlie Chaplin was one of my favorites."[42]

The Harris family went to see *The Learning Tree* by Gordon Parks. Harris said she will never forget the day. "I was interested in watching films, but I didn't see films about me, so it was a real struggle. *The Learning Tree* was the first time I saw images on black people on the screen. I was so happy."[43]

When Harris was in film school, her professors often asked if she wouldn't like to try acting instead. After spending a few years shooting commercials and working for an advertising agency, she decided to attempt a feature. "When I first started raising money for *Just Another Girl on the IRT,* people were laughing at me. The idea of a woman making a feature film was ridiculous. I didn't really wait for Hollywood to come knocking. I did it myself."[44]

JULIE DASH'S BEAUTIFUL VISION

Julie Dash, the director of *Daughters of the Dust,* also knew about the determination and grace that an African American woman in the film industry must have. For ten years Dash was determined to make her film. Set at the turn of the century, *Daughters of the Dust* is the story of a Sunday picnic that the Peazant family holds on their property in the Gullah Islands, located off the coast of Georgia and South Carolina. The inhabitants of these islands are descendants of the Ibo tribe of West Africa. In many ways the group retain their African culture. Their speech, body movements, hair, and dark skin are those of Africans who have not intermingled with whites. The islands held special historical significance. "These islands were a main drop-off point for Africans brought to North America as slaves in the days of the transatlantic slave trade," Dash wrote. "It became the Ellis Island for the Africans, the processing center for the forced immigration of millions." [45]

The clan has decided to leave the island for better opportunities on the mainland. Throughout the day they prepare for one final feast. They all know that they are crossing over from their past into a new beginning. How far will they grow apart from one another? Will this be the last time that they are gathered together? What if the life on the mainland isn't all it's held up to be? Throughout the soul-searching, girls jump rope, boys fish for crabs, women make gumbo, and Nana Peazant tells tales of Africa.

Dash produced and directed a motion picture that is unlike any other in the history of the American screen. It has the sophistication of a foreign film. It is colorful, with long, lingering shots of its characters. It celebrates the beauty of the earth and the beauty of black people. The images that Dash presents of African American women represent a kaleidoscope of skin colors. Their hair is woolly, straight, long, and short. They wear bonnets, braids, dreadlocks, and ponytails. These women do not fit the European definition of beauty. They are beautiful in an African way. The men move in bright white cottons and flowing linens. They are strong. They are vulnerable.

Dash wanted to capture the grace and dignity of the Gullah Islands. Her original screenplay was translated into Gullah by a linguist. The change from standard English to a native tongue has a powerful effect. The words become African poetry, a gumbo of Caribbean, down-home English, and expressions from the Mother Land. "I wrote the film when I was a student at UCLA," Dash said. "I was trying to redefine how we see African American women." [46] As she shopped the film around, executives scratched their heads. They told Dash

THE INTERNATIONALLY ACCLAIMED FILM
DAUGHTERS OF THE DUST, DIRECTED BY
JULIE DASH, TELLS THE STORY OF THE GULLAH PEOPLE ON THE SEA ISLANDS
OFF SOUTH CAROLINA AND GEORGIA AT THE TURN OF THE CENTURY.

that they had never seen a film like the one she was proposing. She didn't care. She, and millions of African Americans, had watched an endless parade of white-oriented and male-oriented screen images. She wanted to produce something different. "When I pitch stories I'm usually talking to a white male," Dash said. "Men want to hear stories about male dramas. So I am asking these executives to extend themselves to look at stories about African American women. They usually disengage from my pitch. They simply aren't interested." [47]

But the international film community was. *Daughters of the Dust* was the toast of foreign film festivals. It was discussed among intellectuals from coast to coast. Some called it a feminist film. Others hailed it as a godsend.

One reason for the film's impact was the stunning visuals of cinematographer Arthur Jafa. (He also shot *Crooklyn* for Spike Lee.) Jafa said he had no trade secrets.

Many people told me that they had never seen black people look so beautiful before. I did not make the actors look beautiful. I cannot give anyone their skin color. I can only appreciate their physical attributes. I can honor them with the camera. I let them be themselves. We played on the environment and the energy. What was different about our film was how we let a group of black people be themselves. There is not one white person in this film. This is about a day of great transition. Some of these people may never see each other again. They're about to scatter. This is about that final day they spent together. Everyone was in their Sunday best. That's how we filmed them.

What we are doing is adapting our visual presence to the technology of filmmaking. Film is still a new medium for us. We did not bring it over here on the slave ship with us. But we will transform film and make it ours. When we master this art, we will turn it upside down. When you think of a saxophone, you think of a pair of black lips and black hands, don't you? Likewise when you say basketball, you think of the black men who have dominated the game. We will take cinema and make it our own. That's just how we are. [48]

The novelist Terry McMillan has a less philosophical view. In 1995 she called the shots with the big-screen adaption of *Waiting to Exhale*, her best-selling novel that deals with the friendship of four successful African American women. McMillan selected Forest Whitaker, the critically acclaimed actor who starred in *Bird, A Rage in Harlem*, and *Jason's Lyric* to direct the film.

Waiting to Exhale, one of the biggest box-office hits of 1995, grossed $65 million. The film was a cultural phenomenon, generating the same level of controversy and discussion provoked a decade earlier by the film version of Alice Walker's *The Color Purple*, directed by Steven Spielberg and starring Whoopi Goldberg, Danny Glover, and Oprah Winfrey. On the hemlines of *Exhale*'s astounding success, at least a half-dozen screenplays and novels by black writers were "optioned" by major Hollywood studios. McMillan sealed

ANGELA BASSETT, DIRECTOR FOREST WHITAKER, AND WHITNEY HOUSTON ON THE SET OF THE 1995 BLOCKBUSTER *WAITING TO EXHALE*.

a $2.5 million deal to write the screenplay for her fourth novel, *How Stella Got Her Groove Back*.

While the author insists that she is simply a writer, others have crowned her as a champion of women and a critic supreme of black men. McMillan resists being placed on such a pedestal. "People keep asking me, 'What is your vision,'" McMillan says, annoyed. "People really take this thing too seriously. *Waiting to Exhale* is just a movie. It would be different if I was rewriting the Ten Commandments. But this is just a movie about four women in America in the 1990s."[49] That's the cold, hard, profitable gospel, according to Terry McMillan.

Epilogue

THE NEW MEDIA GODS

There is total silence in the screening room of Universal Pictures in New York City. Approximately forty journalists and filmmakers have just viewed a rough cut of *Panther*, a political thriller based on the birth and struggles of the Black Panther Party in Oakland, California, during the 1960s. Mario Van Peebles (who is not in attendance) has directed a tense tale of the party's tribulations, tragedies, and battles with the FBI. For ninety minutes the audience had watched a tragedy encompassing America's dark side: poverty, racism, and police brutality. Most entered the screening with one question in mind: How would Van Peebles handle the complex story of a black revolutionary group?

Everyone is spellbound. Occasionally the intensity of the subject matter is broken up with a song from the era like Sly Stone's "Everyday People," which provides a moment of nostalgia. The Afro hairstyles and miniskirts worn by actors on the screen provide some comic relief, but basically the movie doesn't present much to smile about. It is a story about community activists who battle political corruption and oppression. *Panther* is a far cry from *The Birth of a Nation* or *The Birth of a Race*. If it resembles any black-theme motion pictures, it is Spike Lee's *Do the Right Thing* or *Malcolm X*. "I want a picture that moves," Van Peebles said earlier, "that gets right in your face, and yet has those sorts of quiet moments that reveal the characters."[1]

Maestro Pleasants, an aspiring twenty-three-year-old filmmaker, is among the audience that night. As he leaves the screening room, he walks in silence. Finally on a packed elevator he speaks. "This is a story that needs to be told," he says. "It needs to be told so many times. There is not just one story of the Black Panthers. There are many dimensions to that history."[2]

Panther was a moderate success by Hollywood standards, grossing some $20 million since its 1995 release. This liberal dramatization of one of the most militant groups in African American history was challenged by historians and some die-hard, "blacker than black" nationalists, who waved *Panther* off as a romanticized Hollywood formula drama.

The lukewarm reception to *Panther* did not surprise director Van Peebles. Neither *Panther* nor *Posse*, Van Peebles's stellar works to date, brought in as much revenue as his black gangster film, *New Jack City*, which was a $56 million blockbuster. "I really don't make movies for money. I mean, I don't need to buy any more shirts," says Van Peebles. What Van Peebles is most concerned with is the quality of his work. "You may love my work, or you may hate it, but at least you won't forget it."[3]

When Mario talks about his growing-up years, he affectionately refers to his father, director Melvin Van Peebles, as "Melvin Van Movies." While he was always intrigued by films, the young Mario was not starry-eyed about the hard work of moviemaking. He witnessed nightmarish scenes that directors Oscar Micheaux, Robert Townsend, Leslie Harris, Julie Dash, Spike Lee, and Melvin Van Peebles all lived through. "I saw my dad finish a movie with thirteen dollars in his pocket. People were trying to arrest him. People were trying to jump him because he'd broken the [union hiring] rules. I saw him go through a lot of changes. It was like being in a war."[4]

What drives Van Peebles and other filmmakers on a journey that is often uphill and many times thankless? Why does Spike Lee have to fight to make *Malcom X* or *Jackie Robinson*? Why must a major box-office draw like Denzel Washington and a director like Carl Franklin leap through rings of fire to make *Devil in a Blue Dress*?

"Hollywood lies," whispers Van Peebles with a broad, bright cinematic grin. He shakes his head at the contradictions and absurdities that pit African American filmmakers against their Hollywood bosses.

> The masses are spoon-fed and believe...what Hollywood puts out there. Hollywood will tell you that heavyweight champions of the world look like Stallone. But we know that they look like Ali, Tyson, and George Foreman. That's been the reality for years. So, if our grandkids go watch Rocky parts one, two, three, and four, they'll eventually believe that all boxers look like Stallone. So, if you want to make a movie about a brother named Muhammad Ali or Joe Frazier someone will say, "Man, you're trying to revise history."
>
> The dominant culture will put itself in the foreground and will push you into the background. All you have to do is think of anything American. Look at the first charter of Los Angeles. You'll see very clearly that of the first forty-four settlers of Los Angeles, twenty-six of them were black. It was a predominantly African American group. You will not get that reflected in any Western.
>
> You may look at a history book on music, and it may tell you that Vanilla Ice started rap and Benny Goodman started jazz. You may look at a book on sports and read that Larry Bird could dunk. Anytime the other guys write our history, you know what that's going to look like.[5]

Van Peebles believes that black filmmakers have a moral and creative obligation to enlighten the world:

> I am nothing but a conduit. I am blessed to use my few moments in the sun to do some other kind of stuff. Other people might not feel that way, but I do. When you have the opportunity to go where so few of us have

THE NEW GENERATION OF BLACK DIRECTORS: (BACK ROW, FROM LEFT TO RIGHT) MATTY RICH, MARIO VAN PEEBLES, ERNEST DICKERSON, REGINALD HUDLIN, WARRINGTON HUDLIN; (FRONT ROW, FROM LEFT TO RIGHT) SPIKE LEE, JOHN SINGLETON, CHARLES LANE.

gone before, you better put something out that means something. It's like, one of us gets in the kitchen and gets to cook, well cook something good. Don't cook some derivative stuff, cook up something good. That's my agenda. I would be a fool not to use my few moments in the sun. Now the next cat's agenda will be something entirely different.... Give us some other flavors. We need that. [6]

Van Peebles also believes, as do others, that the video age and information superhighway have provided a mere sneak preview of the potential that can be realized by black filmmakers. Mainstream America had little inkling that through technology African American politicians, entertainers, and athletes would become, what Van Peebles dubs, "media gods." In fact, Van Peebles maintains that technology has kicked the black aesthetic, or "the flavor" as he puts it, to a new level of international prominence.

> Years ago when Bill "Bojangles" Robinson was shaking his head and tapping his feet with little Shirley Temple in *The Littlest Colonel*, Hollywood did not anticipate that his descendants like Michael Jordan and Michael Jackson would become America's new media gods.
>
> Anything we get into we take it over. You let us box, brother, you won't get in the ring. You let us play ball, and now we own the NBA. Now when you look at the movies, you have to understand that we don't just have to act or do makeup. We can direct. We can write. We can be cinematographers. We are a very visual people. The seeds have been sown and the precedents have been set for us to expand in the visual arts. [7]

A truly black cinema that is thematically and culturally diverse and technologically innovative remains one of the last frontiers of the entertainment industry for African Americans. As Spike Lee noted, however, conservative and shortsighted media moguls are still resistant. Hollywood remains one of the last bastions of white-dominated cultural decision makers. Frederick Douglass once said that power concedes nothing without demand, and many argue that the demands of black filmmakers are becoming too frequent for Hollywood to continue to ignore.

Van Peebles says that one of the brightest moments of his career was assembling an all-star cast for *Posse*. He was particularly proud of the cameo that he offered to Woody Strode, whose Hollywood performances spanned many decades. Strode starred in race movies like *Bronze Buckaroo* and *Harlem on the Prairie*, working for hand-to-mouth wages (or "the colored actor's pay scale") or playing big bronze extra roles like a tribal chief, a restless native, a submissive slave, and assorted other stereotypes, which paid better money. Van Peebles remembers that when he showed Strode the *Posse* script and asked him to read the opening voice-over for the movie, the elder actor was flabbergasted. The line read, "History is a book written by the winners."

> When Mr. Strode read the script, he said, "They gonna let you say this in the movies, son?" I said, "Yes, sir, this is our movie now, sir." But he said, "But son, you gonna direct this movie? They gonna let you in the editing room? Is the man gonna cut this up?" And I said, "No, sir. This is our movie, sir." He said "I'm in. Count me in."
>
> I told Mr. Strode, "You helped put me here. I am the son of Melvin Van Movies. I am your son. I am Gordon Parks's son. I am Oscar Micheaux's son. I belong to all of you. [8]

In the long history of black filmmakers' often rocky road to acclaim, Spike Lee remains a warrior. Arthur Jafa remains a visionary. Mario Van Peebles remains an optimist. And Oscar Micheaux is the great, great, great grandaddy of them all.

Van Peebles looks out the window onto a spectacular view of Central Park. "We have cursed the darkness and turned on some lights." [9]

nOTES

PROLOGUE
1. *Malcom X.*
2. Author interview with Spike Lee, July 1992, New York.
3. Ibid.
4. Ibid.
5. Ibid.

CHAPTER 1
1. Donald Bogle, *Toms, Coons, Mulattoes, Mammies and Bucks* (New York: Continuum, 1992), p. 4.
2. *Black History, Lost, Stolen, or Strayed*, documentary, CBS News, 1968.
3. Thomas Dixon, *Black Shadows on a Silver Screen*, documentary, Republic Video, 1975.
4. *The American Experience*, "Midnight Ramble," documentary, Public Broadcasting System, 1994.
5. W. E. B. Du Bois, "The Birth of a Nation," *Crisis*, February 1917.
6. *Crisis*, October 1917.
7. *The American Experience*, "Midnight Ramble," op. cit.

8. Ibid.

9. John Hope Franklin, "The Impact of The Birth of a Nation," *All Things Considered*, National Public Radio, July, 1994.

10. Thomas Cripps, *Making Movies Black* (New York: New York University Press, 1993), p. 50.

11. *The American Experience*, "Midnight Ramble," op. cit.

12. *Oscar Micheaux, Film Pioneer*, documentary, Nguzo Saba Films, 1981.

13. *The American Experience*, "Midnight Ramble," op. cit.

14. Ibid.

15. John Kisch and Edward Mapp, *A Separate Cinema: Fifty Years of Black Cast Posters* (New York: The Noon Day Press), p. xx.

16. *Black History, Lost, Stolen, or Strayed*, op. cit.

17. Irene Thirer, "Film Folks Around Town, Facts Concerning Stepin Fetchit and Louise Beaver, Dusky Screen Celebs New Yorking Now," *The New York Evening Post*, February 14, 1935.

18. Author interview with Clayton Riley, October 1994, New York.

19. Irene Thirer, op. cit.

20. Author interview with Matt Robinson, October 1994, New York.

21. "Stepin Fetchit, the First Black to Win Film Fame, Dies at 83," *The New York Times*, November 20, 1985, p. D31.

22. *Paul Robeson: Tribute to an Artist*, documentary, Home Video Entertainment, 1979.

23. Donald Bogle, op. cit., p. 98.

24. *Paul Robeson: Tribute to an Artist*, op. cit.

25. Ibid.

26. James Baldwin, *The Devil Finds Work* (New York: Dial Press, 1976), p. 100.

27. Hattie McDaniel, Academy Award Acceptance Speech, *Daily Variety*, March 1, 1940, p.1.

28. Jerry Tallmer, "Oscar's Story Full of Scuttlebutt & Oddities, Back-of-the-Bus Embarrassment," *New York Post*, March 22, 1986, p.12.

29. Walter White, *A Man Called White* (Bloomington: Indiana University Press, 1970), p. 3.

30. Al Young, "I'd Rather Play a Maid Than Be One," *The New York Times Book Review*, October 15, 1989, p. 13.

31. Hedda Hopper, "Hattie Hates Nobody," *Sunday Chicago Tribune*, December 14, 1947, p. 10.

32. Author interview with Clayton Riley, op. cit.

33. Hedda Harper, op. cit.

CHAPTER 2

1. *The American Experience*, "Midnight Ramble," op. cit.

2. Sidney Poitier, *This Life* (New York: Knopf, 1980), p. 87.

3. Author interview with Matt Robinson, op. cit.

4. Author interview with Clayton Riley, op. cit.

5. Langston Hughes, "Harlem," *The Collected Poems of Langston Hughes* (New York: Knopf, 1994), p. 363.

6. Murray Schumach, "Poitier Wins Oscar as Best Film Actor," *The New York Times*, April 14, 1964, p. 1.

7. Murray Schumach, "Poitier Reflects on Oscar Victory," *The New York Times*, April 15, 1964, p. 1.

8. Ibid.

9. Sidney Poitier, op cit., p. 337.

10. Ibid. pp. 337-338.

CHAPTER 3

1. *Sweet Sweetback's Baadasssss Song*, 1971.

2. Author interview with Warrington Hudlin, March 3, 1987.

3. Bogle, op. cit., p. 238.

4. Roger Ebert, "Gordon Parks Had a Special Dream," *New Jersey Star-Ledger*, July 2, 1972.

5. Isaac Hayes, "The Theme From Shaft," Stax Records, 1971.

6. Gordon Parks, *To Smile in Autumn* (New York: W. W. Norton, 1979), p. 225.

7. Ibid.

8. Author interview with Narcelle Reedus, October 1994, Atlanta.

9. Author interview with Joe Madison, executive director Detroit branch, National Association for the Advancement of Colored People, 1972, Detroit.

10. Sidney Poitier, *This Life*, op. cit., p. 229.

11. Author interview with Durville Martin, Spring 1973, Detroit.

12. Gordon Parks, *To Smile in Autumn*, op. cit., p. 229.

13. Roger Ebert, op. cit.

14. Carla Hall, "With Successes, Black Filmmakers Gain Acceptance," *Washington Post*, September 24, 1991, p. C2.

15. Les Payne, "Richard Pryor's Battle to Find His Own Truth," *Newsday*, June 22, 1980, p. 9.

16. Ibid.

17. Spike Lee, *Spike Lee's Gotta Have It* (New York: Simon & Schuster, 1987), p. 52.

18. David Handleman, "The Last Time We Saw Richard," *Premiere*, January 1992, p. 88.

19. Nelson George, *Black Face* (New York: HarperCollins, 1994), p. 36.

20. Herton, Calvin, ed., *The Collected Stories of Chester Himes* (New York: Thunder's Mouth Press, 1991), p. x.

21. *Buck and the Preacher*, 1971.

22. Ibid.

23. Ibid.

24. Sidney Poitier, *This Life*, op. cit., p. 332.
25. Ibid., pp. 352-353.

CHAPTER 4

1. Author interview with Mrs. Eddie Mae Lewis, September 1994, Birmingham.
2. Author interview with Morehouse alumnus Arthur Kabawtha, Kitwe, Zambia 1989.
3. Author interview with Spike Lee, op. cit.
4. Spike Lee, *Spike Lee's Gotta Have It* (New York: Simon & Schuster, 1987), p. 56.
5. Author interview with Clayton Riley, op. cit.
6. Author interview with Spike Lee, op. cit.
7. Ibid.
8. Ibid.
9. Ibid.
10. *Current Biography*, March 1989, p. 41.
11. Author interview with Morgan Freeman, June 29, 1993, Cleveland.
12. Spike Lee, *By Any Means Necessary; The Trials and Tribulations of Making Malcolm X* (New York: Hyperion, 1992), p. 18.
13. Author interview with Spike Lee, op. cit.
14. Nelson George, "Fort Greene Dreams," *Black Face* (New York: HarperCollins, 1994), p. 80.
15. Author interview with Nicholas Torello, September 1994, New York City.
16. *Hollywood Shuffle*, 1987.
17. Charles Johnson, "One Meaning of Mo' Better Blues," *Five for Five* (New York: Stewart, Tabori and Chang, 1991), pp. 118-119.
18. Zora Neale Hurston, *Their Eyes Were Watching God* (Urbana: University of Illinois Press, 1978), p.1.
19. *She's Gotta Have It*, 1986.
20. *School Daze*, 1988.
21. Author interview with Spike Lee, op. cit.
22. *Do the Right Thing*, 1989.
23. Joe Klein, "The National Interest, Spiked Again," *New York*, June 1, 1992, p. 19.
24. Public Enemy, "Fight the Power," *Fear of a Black Planet* CBS Records, 1989.
25. Cornel West, "Malcolm X and Black Rage," *Race Matters* (Boston: Beacon Press, 1993), p. 95.
26. Michael Wilmington, "Spike Lee's X-Factor," *L.A. Style*, October, 1992, pp. 60-61.
27. James Baldwin, "The Grapes of Wrath," *The Devil Finds Work* (New York: Dial Press, 1976), pp. 96-97.
28. Author interview with Spike Lee, op. cit.

29. James Greenberg, "The Controversy Over *Malcolm X*," *The New York Times*, January 27, 1991, Section H, p. 8.

30. Spike Lee, "The Shoot," *By Any Means Necessary*, p. 98.

31. Ibid, p. 50.

32. Author interview with Spike Lee, op. cit.

33. Ibid.

34. Paul Gilroy, "Fade to Black: How Spike Lee Films Fail Their Audience," *Washington Post*, November 17, 1991, p. C3.

35. Author interview with Spike Lee, op. cit.

36. Ibid.

37. James Baldwin, op. cit., p. 96.

38. Author interview with Spike Lee, op. cit.

39. Ibid.

40. Spike Lee, *By Any Means Necessary*, p. 6.

41. Author interview with Spike Lee, op. cit.

42. Ibid.

43. Author interview with Spike Lee, op. cit.

44. Ibid.

45. Ibid.

46. Kevin Powell, "The Godfather," *Vibe*, June/July 1994, p. 64.

47. William C. Rhoden, "Jackie Robinson, Warrior Hero, Through Spike Lee's Lens," *The New York Times*, October 30, 1994, Section 8, p. 11.

48. Ibid.

CHAPTER 5

1. *American Cinema*, Program 7, "The Independents," Public Broadcasting System, 1995.

2. Author interview with Butch Robinson, November 1994, New York City.

3. Production notes for *The DROP Squad*, p. 4.

4. Author interview with Butch Robinson, op. cit.

5. *The DROP Squad*, 1994.

6. Ibid.

7. Ibid.

8. Author interview with Butch Robinson, op. cit.

9. Author interview with Robert Townsend, February 26, 1987, New York City.

10. Ibid.

11. Ibid.

12. Ibid.

13. Author interview with Cuba Gooding, Jr., February 3, 1992, New York City.

14. Gary Dauphin, "Tales Out of School," *The Village Voice*, January 17, 1995. p. 52.

15. Martha Frankel, "Acerbic Youth, Hughes's Views," *Movieline*, March 1994, p. 65.

16. *Menace II Society*, 1993.

17. Minister Louis Farrakhan, "Let Us Make a Man," sermon, January 1994, New York City.

18. Stephen Rebello, "What's It All About, Alfre?" *Movieline*, May 1994, p. 45.

19. Author interview with Halle Berry, October 1, 1992, New York City.

20. Author interview with Natalie Oliver, December 9, 1995, New York City.

21. *Posse*, 1993.

22. Antonio Sharpe, "Van Peebles Says 'blacks have to direct it like it 'tis,'" *Texas Southern University Herald*, September 1993.

23. Carole R. Simmons, "Hollywood's MVP Playing to Win," *Upscale*, May 1993, p. 34.

24. *House Party* press release, 1989, p. 8.

25. *House Party*, 1989.

26. Author interview with Warrington Hudlin, March 1990, New York City.

27. Nelson George, *Black Face*, op. cit., p. 111.

28. Author interview with Preston Whitmore, November 1994, New York City.

29. Ibid.

30. Ibid.

31. Ibid.

32. Ibid.

33. Ibid.

34. Ibid.

35. Ibid.

36. Ibid.

37. Ibid.

38. Author interview with Leslie Harris, October 29, 1992, Brooklyn.

39. Ibid.

40. Ibid.

41. Ibid.

42. Ibid.

43. Ibid.

44. Ibid.

45. Julie Dash, *Daughters of the Dust: The Making of an African American Woman's Film* (New York: The New Press, 1992), p. 96.

46. Julie Dash interview with Cheryl Chilsom, 1992, Public Broadcasting System.

47. Ibid.

48. Author interview with Arthur Jafa, October 1994, New York City.

49. Author interview with Terry McMillan, August 7, 1995, New York City.

EPILOGUE

1. *Panther* Production notes.
2. Author interview with Maestro Pleasants, March 1995, New York City.
3. Author interview with Mario Van Peebles, January 29, 1996, New York City.
4. Ibid.
5. Ibid.
6. Ibid.
7. Ibid.
8. Ibid.
9. Ibid.

a CHRONOLOGY OF MAJOR FILMS BY AFRICAN AMERICAN DIRECTORS

1925
Body & Soul, Oscar Micheaux

1927
The Scar of Shame, Frank Peregini

1932
Girl from Chicago, Oscar Micheaux

1935
Murder in Harlem, Oscar Micheaux

1938
Swing, Oscar Micheaux

1939
Lying Lips, Oscar Micheaux

1941

Blood of Jesus, Spencer Williams, Jr.

1947

Juke Joint, Spencer Williams, Jr.

1969

The Learning Tree, Gordon Parks, Sr.

1970

Cotton Comes to Harlem, Ossie Davis

1971

Buck and the Preacher, Sidney Poitier
Shaft, Gordon Parks, Sr.
Sweet Sweetback's Baadasssss Song, Melvin Van Peebles

1972

Superfly, Gordon Parks, Jr.

1973

The Legend of Nigger Charlie, Fred Williamson

1974

Uptown Saturday Night, Sidney Poitier

1975

Cooley High, Michael Schultz
Let's Do It Again, Sidney Poitier
Mahogany, Berry Gordy, Jr.

1976

Car Wash, Michael Schultz
Leadbelly, Gordon Parks, Sr.
Which Way Is Up? Michael Schultz

1977

A Piece of the Action, Sidney Poitier
Greased Lightning, Michael Schultz

1980
Stir Crazy, Sidney Poitier

1986
She's Gotta Have It, Spike Lee
Jo Jo Dancer, Your Life is Calling, Richard Pryor

1987
Hollywood Shuffle, Robert Townsend

1988
I'm Gonna Git You Sucka, Keenan Ivory Wayans
School Daze, Spike Lee

1989
Do the Right Thing, Spike Lee
House Party, Hudlin Brothers

1990
Jungle Fever, Spike Lee
Mo' Better Blues, Spike Lee
To Sleep with Anger, Charles Burnett

1991
Boyz N the Hood, John Singleton
Daughters of the Dust, Julie Dash
The Five Heartbeats, Robert Townsend
New Jack City, Mario Van Peebles
One False Move, Carl Franklin
Straight Out of Brooklyn, Matty Rich

1992
Boomerang, Hudlin Brothers
Juice, Ernest Dickerson
Just Another Girl on the IRT, Leslie Harris
Malcolm X, Spike Lee

1993

Bopha!, Morgan Freeman
Menace II Society, Hughes Brothers
Meteor Man, Robert Townsend
Posse, Mario Van Peebles
A Rage in Harlem, Bill Duke

1994

Crooklyn, Spike Lee
The DROP Squad, Butch Robinson
I Like It Like That, Darnell Martin
Jason's Lyric, McHenry-Jackson
The Inkwell, Matty Rich
Poetic Justice, John Singleton
Sugar Hill, Leon Ichaso

1995

Clockers, Spike Lee
Dead Presidents, Hughes Brothers
Devil in a Blue Dress, Carl Franklin
Panther, Mario Van Peebles
Tales from the Hood, Rusty Aundiezz
Waiting to Exhale, Forest Whitaker

1996

Don't Be a Menace to South Central, Shawn Wayans
Fled, Kevin Hooks
Girl 6, Spike Lee
The Great White Hope, Reginald Hudlin
Thin Line Between Love and Hate, Martin Lawrence

A CHRONOLOGY OF OTHER IMPORTANT FILMS AND DOCUMENTARIES

1903
Uncle Tom's Cabin (short), William R. Daley

1914
The Birth of a Nation, D. W. Griffith
Uncle Tom's Cabin, William R. Daley

1929
Hallelujah, King Vidor

1933
The Emperor Jones, Dudley Murphy

1936
The Green Pastures, William Keighley and Marc Connelly
Show Boat, James White

1939
Gone With the Wind, Victor Fleming

1943
Cabin in the Sky, Vincente Minnelli
Stormy Weather, Andrew Stone

1952
Cry, the Beloved Country, Zaltan Korda

1954
Carmen Jones, Otto Preminger

1958
St. Louis Blues, Robert Smith

1961
A Raisin in the Sun, Daniel Petrie

1963
Lilies of the Field, Ralph Nelson

1965
Nothing But a Man, Michael Roemer

1970
The Great White Hope, Martin Ritt

1972
Lady Sings the Blues, Sidney J. Furie
Sounder, Martin Ritt

1973
Black Caesar, Larry Cohen
Cleopatra Jones, Jack Starreet
Coffy, Jack Hill
The Harder They Come, Perry Henzell
The Mack, Michael Campus

1974
Claudine, John Berry

1976

Bingo Long Traveling All-Stars and Motor Kings, John Badham

1978

The Wiz, Sidney Lumet

1982

An Officer and a Gentleman, Taylor Hackford
48 Hours, Walter Hill

1984

Beverly Hills Cop, Martin Brent
The Brother From Another Planet, John Sayles
Purple Rain, Albert Magnoli
A Soldier's Story, Norman Jewison
Sugar Cane Alley, Euzhan Palcy

1985

The Color Purple, Steven Spielberg

1986

Round Midnight, George Bertrand Taverner

1987

Cry Freedom, Richard Attenborough

1988

Coming to America, John Landis

1989

A Dry White Season, Euzhan Palcy
Driving Miss Daisy, Bruce Beresford
Glory, Edward Zick

1991

City of Hope, John Sayles
Mississippi Masala, Mira Nair
Young Soul Rebels, Issac Julien

1992

Sarafina!, Darrell Rodt

1993

What's Love Got to Do With It, Brian Gibson

1994

Cool Runnings, Jon Turteltaub
Hoop Dreams (documentary), Steve James

1995

Cry, the Beloved Country, Darrell Roodt
Othello, Oliver Parker
Sankofa, Haille Gerima
White Man's Burden, Desmond Nakano

1996

Ghost of Mississippi, Rob Reiner
Gone Fishin', Chris Kain
Kazaam, Paul Michael Glaser
Original Gansta', Larry Cohen
Race the Sun, Charlie Kinganis
Solo, Norbeto Barba
Space Jam, Joe Pytka
The Nutty Professor, Tom Shadyac

ABOUT FILM AND FILMMAKERS

American Cinema, Public Television Broadcasting, 1995
Black History, Lost, Stolen, or Strayed, narrated by Bill Cosby, CBS News,1968.
Black Shadows on a Silver Screen, narrated by Ossie Davis, Republic Video, 1975.
Gordon Parks' Visions, Past America, Inc., 1991.
Oscar Micheaux, Film Pioneer, Nguzo Saba Films, 1981.
Paul Robeson: Tribute to an Artist, narrated by Sidney Poitier, Home Vision Entertainment, 1979.
That's Black Entertainment, Skyline Productions, 1989.
The American Experience, "Midnight Ramble," Public Television Broadcasting, 1994.

Sources

Andrews, Bert, and Paul Carter Harrison. *In the Shadow of the Great White Way: Images from the Black Theater.* New York: Thunder's Mouth Press, 1989.

Baldwin, James. *The Devil Finds Work.* New York: Dial Press, 1976.

Bogle, Donald. *Brown Sugar: Eighty Years of America's Black Female Superstars.* New York: Crown Publishers, 1980.

Bogle, Donald. *Toms, Coons, Mulattoes, Mammies and Bucks.* New York: Continuum, 1993.

Breitman, George. *Malcolm X Speaks.* New York: Grove Weidenfeld, 1965.

Chapnick, Howard, ed. *Malcolm X, The Great Photographs.* New York: Stewart, Tabori and Chang, 1993.

Cook, David A. *A History of Narrative Film.* New York: W. W. Norton, 1981.

Cripps, Thomas. *Making Movies Black: The Hollywood Message Movie from World War II to the Civil Rights Era.* New York: Oxford University Press, 1993.

Dash, Julie (with Toni Cade Bambara and bell hooks). *Daughters of the Dust: The Making of an African American Woman's Film.* New York: The New Press, 1992.

Du Bois, Shirley Graham. *Du Bois: A Pictorial Biography.* Chicago: Johnson Publishing , 1978.

Dyson, Michael Eric. *Between God and Gangster Rap.* New York: Oxford University Press, 1996.

————. *Reflecting Black*. Minneapolis: University of Minnesota Press, 1993.

Facets African American Video Guide. Chicago: Facets Multimedia, Inc., 1994.

George, Nelson. *Black Face*. New York: HarperCollins, 1994.

George, Nelson. *Buppies, B-Boys, Baps, and Bohos*. New York: HarperCollins, 1992.

Guerrero, Ed. *Framing Blackness: The African American Image in Film*. Philadelphia: Temple University Press, 1993.

Herton, Calvin, ed. *The Collected Stories of Chester Himes*. New York: Thunder's Mouth Press, 1991.

Hurston, Zora Neale. *Their Eyes Were Watching God*. Urbana: University of Illinois Press, 1978.

Kisch, John, and Edward Mapp. *A Separate Cinema: Fifty Years of Black Cast Posters*. New York: The Noon Day Press, 1992.

Leab, Daniel, J. *From Sambo to Superspade*. Boston: Houghton Mifflin Company, 1976.

Lee, David, and Spike Lee. *The Films of Spike Lee: Five for Five*. New York: Stewart, Tabori and Chang, 1991.

Lee, Spike (with Ralph Wiley). *By Any Means Necessary: The Trials and Tribulations of Making Malcolm X*. New York: Hyperion, 1992.

Lee, Spike. *Spike Lee's Gotta Have It: Inside Guerrilla Filmmaking*. New York: Simon & Schuster, 1987.

Null, Gary. *Black Hollywood: From 1970 to Today*. New York: Citadel Press, 1993.

Parks, Gordon. *To Smile in Autumn*. New York: W. W. Norton, 1979.

Patterson, Lindsay. *Black Films and Film Makers*. New York: Dodd, Mead, and Company, 1975.

Poitier, Sidney. *This Life*. New York: Knopf, 1980.

Pryor, Richard. *Pryor Convictions*. New York: Pantheon Books, 1995.

Schacter, Susan, and Don Shewey. *Caught in the Act: New York Actors Face to Face*. New York: New American Library, 1986.

Strickland, Bill, and Cheryll Y. Greene, eds. *Malcolm X: Make It Plain*. New York: Viking Press, 1994.

Taraborrelli, Randy J. *Motown*. New York: Dolphin Books, 1986.

Turner, Patricia A. *Ceramic Uncles and Celluloid Mammies: Black Images and Their Influence on Culture*. New York: Anchor Books, 1994.

Ukadike, Nwachukwu Frank. *Black African Cinema*. Berkeley, Los Angeles, and London: University of California Press, 1994.

West, Cornel. *Race Matters*. Boston: Beacon Press, 1993.

White, Walter. *A Man Named White*. Bloomington and London: Indiana University Press, 1970.

Woods, Joe, ed. *Malcolm X: In Our Image*. New York: St. Martin's Press, 1992.

INDEX